THE STAR IN MY HEART

Experiencing Sophia, Inner Wisdom

BY JOYCE RUPP

San Diego, California

LuraMedia ™

© Copyright 1990 LuraMedia
San Diego, California
International Copyright Secured
Publisher's Catalog Number LM-622
Printed and bound in the United States of America

Front and back cover design, and chapter title pages by Carol Jeanotilla, Denver, CO.
Printed on recycled paper.

LuraMedia
7060 Miramar Road, Suite 104
San Diego, CA 92121

Library of Congress Cataloging-in-Publication Data
Rupp, Joyce.
    The star in my heart : experiencing Sophia, inner wisdom / by Joyce Rupp.
        p.   cm. — (The Women's series)
    Includes bibliographical references.
    ISBN 0-931055-75-X
    1. Women—Religious life. 2. Wisdom (Biblical character)
3. Christian life—1960– 4. Rupp, Joyce. I. Title. II. Series: Women's series (San
Diego, Calif.)
BV4527.R86   1990
248—dc20   90-41108
                                                                         CIP

Grateful acknowledgment is made to the following copyright holders for permission to use their copyrighted material:

Addison-Wesley Publishing Company, Inc., for the quotation from TRANSITIONS: MAK-
ING SENSE OF LIFE'S CHANGES by William Bridges. Copyright © 1980 by Addison-
Wesley Publishing Company, Inc., Reading, MA. Reprinted by permission of the publisher.

Ballantine Books, for the quotation from NECESSARY LOSSES by Judith Viorst. Copyright
© 1986 by Judith Viorst. Published by Ballantine books by arrangement with Simon and
Schuster, Inc. Used by permission.

Doubleday and Company, Inc., for the following quotations:
        From THE JERUSALEM BIBLE. Copyright © 1966 by Darton, Longman & Todd,
        Ltd. and Doubleday, a division of Bantam, Doubleday, Dell Publishing Group, Inc.
        Reprinted by permission.
        From "Hagia Sophia," A THOMAS MERTON READER, edited by Thomas
        McDonell, Image Books. Copyright © 1974 by Doubleday, a division of Bantam,
        Doubleday, Dell Pubblishing Group, Inc. Reprinted by permission of the publisher.

Pantheon Books, for quotations from AN INTERRUPTED LIFE: THE DIARIES OF ETTY
HILLESUM, 1941–43 by Etty Hillesum. Copyright © 1981 by De Haan/Uniebock b.v.,
Bussum. English translation copyright © 1983 by Jonathan Cape Ltd. Used by permission of
Pantheon Books, a division of Random House, Inc.

Sheed and Ward, for quotations from SELECTED POETRY OF JESSICA POWERS by Jessica
Powers, edited by Regina Siegfried, Robert Morneau. Copyright © 1989 by Sheed and Ward.
Used by permission of Sheed and Ward.

Acknowledgments

As I wrote this book, Sophia led me to so many helpful people and situations. I have not written this book alone. Many people joined me by their information, their support and prayer, their suggestions and comments, their places of quiet and solitude. I am especially grateful to the following:

- Lura Jane Geiger, whose invitation to write for the LuraMedia Women's Series challenged me and encouraged me.

- Elizabeth Ann Schmidt, a beautiful child who unknowingly elicited my decision to write about my experiences of Sophia.

- Mary F. Kunkel, Claudette McDonald, P. J. McDonald, JoDee Rottler, and Catherine Rupp,osm, for their many hours of reading the chapters and offering helpful criticisms.

- Vince Burns, Sharon and Scott Samek, and Tom Pfeffer, for the blessing of their ocean and mountain homes and the solitude of the wooded parks of rural Iowa where much of this book was written.

- Howard Anderson, who gifted me with my childhood memory of the stars.

- Delmarie Gibney, Mary Katherine Fogarty, Carrie Kirsch, and Maria Friedman, from the FSPA community and Jim Polich for their helpful information and resourcing.

- Jean Sitter,rsm, and the women who gathered at Knowles-Mercy Retreat Center; the ASC community of Ruma, Illinois, who brought me to a wonderful group of missionaries in West Africa; these groups prayed and reflected on my insights about Sophia and greatly confirmed my experiences of her.

- Windsor Heights Lutheran Church, especially pastor Dick Rehfeldt, whose invitation to use their office space has blessed me many times; and to other staff members whose welcome has sustained me in my busy days: pastor Norm Litzner, Eileen Jaschen, Shirley Meese, Mary McBride, and Bev Henderson.

- Bishop Maurice Dingman, whose hopeful presence in the Church has sustained my own faith journey in times of disenchantment.

- Ruth Butler, a special gift to me as editor. Ruth's gracious way of befriending Sophia has given me great joy.

- My brothers and sisters, my Servite community, my friends, and all those who have gathered at retreats and conferences with me; their support, affirmation, and insights have been a great source of help to me.

- The person I most want to thank is Sophia. I would never have written this book without her light in my heart and in the hearts of all those whom I have mentioned here. Thank you, Sophia, for being the Star for us!

I prayed, and understanding was given me;
I entreated, and the spirit of Wisdom came to me.
I esteemed her more than scepters and thrones;
compared with her, I held riches as nothing.
I reckoned no priceless stone to be her peer,
for compared with her, all gold is a pinch of sand,
and beside her silver ranks as mud.
I loved her more than health or beauty,
preferred her to the light,
since her radiance never sleeps.
In her company all good things came to me,
at her hands riches not to be numbered.
I determined to take her to share my life,
knowing she would be my counsellor in prosperity,
my comfort in cares and sorrow.

Wisdom 7:7-11, 8:9

Contents

When we grow in wisdom, we often do so by going within to
the darkness of our inner depths. Sophia is the Star who
guides us and protects us on this journey.

One of the wisdoms that we come to as we go inward is the
recognition of how closely connected we are to the whole
earth. Sophia bonds us to all of life.

As we grow older, Sophia takes us inside to places where we
would rather not go. She urges us to let go of old, worn-out
beliefs that stifle our growth.

Deep within us there are leftover hurts and memories etched
with sharp edges of pain. Sophia companions us toward
wholeness in a slowly evolving process.

A storehouse of memories dwells inside the wonder of who
we are. Sophia smiles upon us and blesses us with joy and
hope as we reflect and gather strength from these memories.

When Sophia gifts us with truth she keeps drawing us to the
open window of life, where we can fly freely and accept more
of the truth of who we truly are.

Sophia encourages us to continue in pursuit of her treasures
and to believe in the power of the Star dwelling within one's
very self.

For Hilda,

my mother and friend,

In gratitude

for the Starlight

in her heart.

My Journey to Wisdom

*Once upon a time a child of happiness
danced upon the land, knew friendship
with the earth and celebrated life with
her love of solitude and simple things.*

*She grew into a young woman, whose
vision of self was clouded, clothed
with the complexities of insecurity
and the necessity of leaving the
hallowed womb of the quiet earth.
She walked into cities of strangers,
straining her inner eye to catch
the slightest hint of the beauty that
had energized her younger days
when she played upon the earth.*

*Days stretched into months and then
years went by. She slowly changed
by going deeper, deeper, into her Center.
Never understanding why the desire to
go deeper was there but always knowing
there was no other choice than to follow
at all cost. Darkness often loomed
up large against her searching journey.
Risk and Truth became her companions.
She met Compassion and then Wisdom
came to greet her.*

*So close, at times, were these companions
that she wept for their intensity and her
unworthiness. Still they walked with her,
and everywhere she went, her companions
reached out and blessed the people of her
life. She could only kneel in gratitude,
offering her heart of praise to the Divine
Companion who had faithfully kept the kindling
of love burning in her heart.*

— Joyce Rupp

Thoughts from the Author

This book was born on a sunny day as I sat among the myriad colors and fragrances of my friends' rose garden. I was watching over their two-year-old Elizabeth Ann who was delightfully playing among the flowers, talking to them, laughing, and splashing the roses with her little watering can. It was there that I became keenly aware of Sophia's presence. I looked at the beautiful child at play, and I remembered how Sophia (Wisdom) speaks of herself in Proverbs:

> I was at God's side . . .
> delighting God day after day,
> ever at play in God's presence,
> at play everywhere in God's world . . .
>   Proverbs 8:30–31

It was not the first time that I had experienced this deep awareness of Sophia's presence. There had been many moments in my life when the sudden recognition of her radiant presence had pressed tears into my eyes. Oftentimes it happened when I looked upon something in nature and felt a wordless connection between the vast beauty of the universe and the goodness of Divine life.

This kind of recognition happened when I saw Elizabeth at play. In an instant all the years that stretched between Elizabeth's age and my own were connected. I saw how Sophia had touched my heart time and again and had brought me to truths that had indeed changed my life. Marveling at Sophia's presence, I took up my pen and began to piece together my proposal for LuraMedia. I knew then that I wanted to write about Sophia's presence in my life. I wanted to tell how her activity in my spirit has led me to many truths which now inspire my life's journey and give order to my inner being.

For many years I have had a file folder labeled "wisdom." It began by my being intrigued with the wisdom literature of the Hebrew scriptures.[1] I found many verses there that connected to my own story. In the poetry of those scriptures, Wisdom is referred to as "she," a rather exceptional event in a strongly male-dominated world. In many cultures of the past, including Egyptian, Babylonian, and Chinese, wisdom was considered to be something very practical, a means of moral values as well as to right living which is given in maxims and proverbs. In the Hebrew scriptures wisdom is also associated with guidance, but there is a wonderful addition: Wisdom becomes alive. Wisdom becomes a person, a "she." This feminine wisdom is presented as one who not only gives us direction for our lives but is intimately bonded with God. She is a breath of the Divine, born before creation; her origin contains great mystery.[2] She is given to humankind to connect them with the Divine. Wisdom is a unique manifestation of God, a catalyst for transformation of the human person's life into one of light and goodness. This is the way she is described in the book of Wisdom:

> Within her is a spirit intelligent, holy,
> unique, manifold, subtle,
> active, incisive, unsullied,
> lucid, invulnerable, benevolent, sharp,
> irresistible, beneficent, loving to humankind,
> steadfast, dependable, unperturbed,
> almighty, all-surveying,
> penetrating all intelligent, pure
> and most subtle spirits;
> for Wisdom is quicker to move than any motion;
> she is so pure, she pervades and permeates all things.
> She is a breath of the power of God,
> pure emanation of the glory of the Almighty;
> hence nothing impure can find a way into her.
> She is a reflection of the eternal light,
> untarnished mirror of God's active power,
> image of God's goodness.
> Wisdom 7:22-26

When I discovered that the Greek word for Wisdom is "Sophia," she took on a very personal and intimate connection for me. This discovery bonded me to her in a profound way. Wisdom took on the shape of a trusted companion, yearning for my good, believing in me, blessing me with surprising elements of growth. I began to see how Sophia had always been there for me, leading me to the discovery of Truth. I saw with greater clarity than ever before how I had long traveled in the inner realms of my self because of Sophia's presence.

As I reflected upon Sophia's place in my own spiritual journey, I determined not to have this book be another intellectual study about wisdom but rather to approach it in Sophia's way, through the feminine, i.e., the heart, one's lived experience as it is integrated in the totality of one's being. To do this has meant that I have had to be reflective, quiet, take time to go inward, to meet my self in loving attention, to listen to the ways that Sophia has been present to me and I to her. It has been a quest made in awe and with reverence, knowing that Sophia is a loving presence, ever ready to reveal. It is my own restlessness, fear, doubt, and hesitation that I have had to struggle with as I searched to name her presence in my life.

Thomas Merton speaks of Sophia as "my sister." He also describes her as "the Child who is a prisoner in all the people, and who says nothing. She smiles, for though they have bound her, she cannot be a prisoner. Not that she is strong, or clever but simply that she does not understand imprisonment."[3] I do not know when Sophia was set free in me. It has been happening for a long, long time. Perhaps she first found freedom in the early years of my youth, when I was Elizabeth's age, as I spent many hours in a wooded grove of trees, at peace as I delighted in the earth-things which have such powerful and positive energy for me. I only know that as I looked upon the play of Elizabeth among the roses that tears of gratitude came to my eyes. They were tears that recognized how long Wisdom has been my sister and my companion through the dark places. For it is in those dark places that I have learned the most wondrous of truths and have found inner freedom and serenity.

These inner truths and wisdoms that now are influencing my attitudes and guiding my life's decisions are the content of the following chapters. These chapters will always be incomplete and unfinished because there are still so many discoveries to be made with Sophia by my side. It is with a strong recognition of my own frailty that I offer you the gathering of wisdoms on the following pages . . . "knowing I could not master wisdom but by the gift of God, a mark of understanding to know whose the bounty was" (Wisdom 8:21).

I share my discovered wisdoms with you in order to encourage you on your own inner way and to spark the recognition of your wisdoms that are waiting to be welcomed by you. At the end of each chapter you will find suggestions for going inward, for meeting Sophia in your own heart. My hope is that you will gather the gift of time and take the journey to the inner world where Sophia waits for you.

— *Joyce Rupp*

Thoughts from the Artist

I have designed a mandala for each chapter of *The Star in My Heart*. My hope is that it will be helpful to ponder these sacred circles in the light of the chapter's content and your own life experiences.

Mandala is a Sanskrit word meaning "to have possession of one's essence." It is a sacred circle with a centerpoint, a universal image that has long been a source of the experience of oneness and wisdom. It uses symbolic forms to draw out truth from the unconscious. These symbols help connect our inner life to our outer life.

The making of the mandala requires from us an attitude of receptivity and reverence. It is a search for and a recording of our deepest self at one moment in time and serves as a container for our deepest emotions. A mandala may be drawn, painted, sculpted, and even danced. It may involve recognizable symbols or it may take an abstract form.

To begin the mandala, it is often helpful to have soft, meditative music in the background. You will need to have paper or a journal page, a pencil and compass for making the circle guide, crayons, Cray-Pas™, pastels, markers, or paints.

Find a quiet place where you will not be disturbed for about thirty minutes. Close your eyes for a few minutes and become aware of your breathing. With each breath, let go of concerns, centering on the experience.

Open your eyes and look at the colors in front of you. Remembering that being receptive is important, allow a color to "choose you." Begin at the center of the mandala with whatever form suggests itself to you. Work outward from the center. When you are finished with your mandala, you may wish to write about it, date it, and give it a title.

— *Judith Veeder*

INTRODUCTION

Wisdom Calls Aloud in the Streets,
She Raises Her Voice in the Public Squares;
She Calls Out at the Street Corners,
She Delivers Her Message at the City Gates.

PROVERBS 1:20-21

How can I hear Sophia's voice in the busyness of my days? Proverbs assures me that she is everywhere, calling out to me. How can this powerful source of inner light and guidance be discovered and received? From my experience I believe that Sophia is most always heard if I allow my knowledge, insights, and events to gestate in my heart. This means that I must have some solitude for reflection. Taking time for this has been an ongoing struggle and tension in my life. I know intellectually that I must have time, space, and quiet in order to have this gestation occur. I yearn for this time, but my life gets so full, so busy, that I never seem to "have enough" of the time for solitude and quiet that I long for and need. Yet, when I am faithful to setting aside enough deliberate time for reflection, I find that my spirit is much more attuned to hear Sophia's voice throughout the whole of the day. Because Sophia is "a breath of the power of God . . . a reflection of the eternal light . . . more splendid than the sun," she can give light and perspective on the things that stir and struggle in my heart (Wisdom 7:25-26,29).

The quiet spaces in my life are necessary if there is to be a movement from the head to the heart, for it is in the heart that wisdoms are born. I can know and experience many things, but they remain only knowledge until I allow them to sink into the depths of my heart, there to toss and to turn, to weep and to wail, to leap and to dance. Sophia helps me to take facts, data, events, experiences, down into my spiritual womb. There they sit in me, gestate, and are transformed into truths which are eventually brought up into the light of my consciousness. These discovered truths give my life a right ordering, where the best of who I am can come to be realized.

Sophia is a lifegiving energy in my spirit. She guides me as I look back on my life, enabling me to see in a different light what I have taken to be only pain and anguish. Sophia also helps me to taste and to relish blessings that tumble unexpectedly in my most common moments. It is Sophia who causes me to hear in my life's journey the sounds of One who calls me farther, deeper, longer, purer, than I ever imagined possible. It is she who guards and guides me, smelling the danger and the smoke of annihilation in my false decisions, wrong turns and confused times. And it is Sophia who draws me to touch into the heart of love, pleading with me to not be so afraid of losing a part of myself in the process.

Sophia coaxes, urges, encourages me to come into the deep recesses where I have not yet been transformed. She guides me inward, saying, "Do not fear; be of great courage; you will find blessings for your spirit in these dark places of your deepest self. You will bring them up into the light and discover that they are your greatest treasures."

That is why it is so necessary to accept the gift of time for reflection and to find a quiet space where I can go on a very regular basis. I need to be there with my hopes high, believing that Sophia, the Divine Light, is always there, filling my darkness, urging me on to growth. I believe that this is true for all of us. She never leaves us and she waits, giving us the time we need to discover the wonders and the wisdoms of who we are and how we are connected to all of life.

As we accept this gift of time for reflection, we will each discover our style or form of meditation. It will vary and change as our lives are slowly transformed. For some of us the best way to grow into our wisdoms will be to walk them out, alone with the earth, perhaps in the vitality of dawn or under a star-shaped sky. For others it will be having both feet firmly planted in the scriptures; yet, for others, the use of a mantra (the repetition of a sacred word or phrase), or the drawing of a mandala, or the process of music making, song or dance, or maybe some hours with a fishing pole in our hands sitting beside the quiet waters of our favorite lake. However it is that we choose to reflect, to go inward, the significant thing is that we do so, that we are without words for a time, that we are not focused on "doing" and that we are willing to be without cozy feelings or a sense of direction for awhile.

Sophia knows the way in which we need to go: "She led them by a marvellous road; she herself was their shelter by day and their starlight through the night" (Wisdom 10:17). It is up to us to listen to the guidance of Sophia as we pause in those quiet places. She will gift us by giving us her children, the wisdoms of our heart.

CHAPTER ONE
THE STAR IN MY HEART

Wisdom is Bright and Does Not Grow Dim.
By Those Who Love Her She is Readily Seen,
and Found by Those Who Look For Her.

WISDOM 6:12

Sophia,
to you I come:
you are the Wisdom of God
you are the Whirl of the Spirit
you are the Intimate Connection
you are the Star in my Heart

Sophia,
open my being to the radiance of your presence
to the guidance of your companionship
to the compassion of your indwelling
to the lighting of your blessed vision

Sophia, trusted friend, beloved companion,
Sophia,
mercy-maker, truth-bearer, love-dweller,
Sophia,
all goodness resides within you.

Sophia,
take me by the hand
bless the frailty of my weak places
strengthen my ability to dwell in darkness
for it is there that your deepest secrets are revealed.

Sophia,
we walk together!

— Joyce Rupp

The stars have long been earth companions for me. Since I was a child I have looked at the night skies and loved what I saw there. Something about the stars radiates hope in my heart and draws me far beyond my little space of earth. An old family friend told me that one evening he and his wife had come to visit my mother and father after we children were all safely tucked into bed. Late in the evening they heard a rustle in the kitchen, and they found me standing by the window. When they asked me why I wasn't in bed, I said very plainly in my three-year-old voice, "Oh, I just wanted to come down and look at the stars." Hearing this story made me wonder if my love of the stars was perhaps born at that very early age. It certainly confirmed my deep connection with these radiant friends of the universe.

As an adult I have kept my fondness for the stars and feel a special leap of delight when I pause in a wintry evening to see the strong and bold marks of Orion in the sky. Or on a summer's night, to walk along and gaze up at the community of light in the Pleiades. I feel that the stars bless me with their presence. There have been times in the midst of deep pain in my heart that I have walked under the night sky and cried out to God, "By the light of your stars, heal me." There is something extremely consoling about walking in great darkness and having the light of the stars to guide the way. After a walk under the stars, light eventually returns to my darkened spirit. The healing that I need comes in future days (or months!) through people, books, sacred moments, music, insights, all of which clarify my confusion and soften the pain in my heart.

I like to think of Sophia as a star in my heart, one whose light guides me and consoles me in my inner darkness, drawing me to a bondedness with a greater truth than I presently know or understand. No matter how hard I fight to stay "in the light," I will have some darkness in my life. This is as sure as the pattern of sunrise and sunset in the natural course of the day. My darkness comes from many sources, sometimes from the pain and struggle of changing ideas, relationships or work, or from my participation in the human condition of aging, accidents, and illness. It has also come from that silent journey when I have desired to be more united with the Divine who is the beloved one dwelling at the center of who I am. This calls for the risky journey into the depths of my self because, most

4

often, the way to the Divine is one of going through the passage of darkness within, having only the glimmer of Sophia's light to tend the way.

The Divine is also discovered in my happy, joyous, light-filled times, but no matter how much light I carry within me, there will always be times of feeling lost, being confused, seeking direction. It is the way of the human heart. It is the way of going inward. It is the way of Sophia.

At times I have found it difficult to believe that darkness could be a source of growth. Darkness to a child, as well as to many adults, can be a scary, fearsome place where wild creatures wait to pounce and prey. But, in actuality, some kinds of darkness are truly our friends. The world of our mother's womb had no light: It is where we grew wonderfully and filled out our tiny limbs of life. Our earth would be quite lifeless, too, if we did not plant seeds deep within the lonely darkness of the soil so they could germinate and bring forth green shoots. I know, too, that we would soon die of an overheated planet if nightfall did not come to soothe the sunfilled land. Darkness is very essential for some aspects of growth and protection.

But there is also an unfriendly darkness, like human destructiveness or hate, a blackness that can maim and wound us mentally, emotionally, spiritually. It is the kind that will lead us to despair, where we end up hurting ourselves or others. It destroys our hope and our positive view of life. We do not grow in this kind of darkness. We turn in on self. We stop believing in our goodness and beauty and that of others.

How do I know what kind of darkness to stay in? It is not easy to know. Sometimes I just do not know. I always need someone to walk faithfully with me during these times of darkness. Sophia's light and guidance are present to me through my human companions. A spiritual guide or a counseling companion is a great blessing at such a time. If at all possible, I need to find these people and welcome them into my life. If I call on Sophia, she will lead me to these companions.

I will need to wait the darkness out, say it out, pray it out. Eventually, I will know what kind of darkness it is by the effects that it has on my life and on the lives of those around me. If it brings life (new hope, greater understanding, more courage, deeper trust . . .), the darkness is my friend. I believe that almost all of my darkness is lifegiving if I have Sophia with me. Jessica Powers understood this when she wrote: "God sits on a chair of darkness in my soul."[4] Sophia is my Star to light up what seems to be an unbearable or impossible passage of life. I may not want to believe that darkness can be growthful because ache, loneliness, hurt, hollowness are not feelings that I enjoy. Yet, if I look back on my life, to those dark times, I can see that I have, or could have, grown deeper and wiser from my experience of the darkness.

I remember a passageway in my life, twenty years ago, when I was far from home for the first time. I lived with people I did not know. I taught school in a place I did not like. I felt a tremendous loneliness like a black cloud over me day after day. I felt sad and empty all the time. I could not imagine how this darkness would be good for me. All I wanted to do was to run away from it. But I had accepted a teaching position and I felt a responsibility to stay.

This experience ended up being one of the best things that ever happened to me. I call those years of loneliness my "island years" because it was then that I learned to live with myself. After several months of intense sadness something in me nudged me to go to the woods regularly to ponder life. At first when I went there I only felt my loneliness. Eventually I began to learn from it. My loneliness was saying to me, "Spend time with yourself. Don't run away." I began to see how afraid I was of myself, how fearful I was to look inside. As I was drawn to go within, I discovered to my great surprise that there was goodness and beauty there. I learned, too, that I was not alone. I began sensing the companionship of God dwelling within me. I did not know Sophia then, but now I see that it was she who guided me during that dark time. It was she who led me through my fears and loneliness. It was Sophia who held my hand and drew me to her light within me.

There is a story told in the Christian scriptures of three astrologers who followed an immensely bright star (Matthew 2:1–12). They were so drawn by this star that they followed a hunch in their hearts that it would lead them to the Divine. So set were their hearts on this bright vision in the sky that they pursued it over great distances and through many struggles. Following the star meant that they had to do their traveling at night. They did not know where they would be led. They only knew that they had to follow. They lost sight of the star, and in great humility, they had to rely on other starseekers to tell them where to locate the star again.

This star "filled their hearts with delight" (Matthew 2:10). They continued to follow it in the darkness of the night, journeying until finally they found themselves at the feet of the one whom they had long sought. Surely Sophia must have danced a radiant star dance on that night when these weary travelers finally reached the goal of their long journey.

This story is so like my own inner one. I feel drawn to seek the Divine. I go mostly in the night, not being sure of the direction, or of what this God will look like, or where the journey will take me. I lose my way. Then I find others who have seen the star. They show me and guide me. I find the way again. And one day I discover God as the beloved, the one for whom I have so yearned. This may be in the most unlikely of places, and perhaps just for a fleeting moment, but I know in that brief discovery that the journey has been worth it. My heart, like those seekers of long ago, is filled with delight. This discovery is usually a very brief experience. And so I continue on the journey of life with hope in my heart, seeking by the light of the star to have another glimpse of the beloved.

This is the way of those who choose to know Sophia and to pursue her secrets, the secrets of wisdom that lead to wholeness of life, to peace of heart.

I love the Star in my heart. She has taken my hand so often and has led me through the dark times. I believe that she is a companion through the darkness for all of us. She helps us to not be so afraid and to trust in our journey to the inner places which we have yet to visit. It is good for us to remember this truth in our dark times for Sophia is "bright and does not grow dim. By those who love her she is readily seen, and found by those who look for her" (Wisdom 6:12).

★

Here are some of the wisdoms I am finding with Sophia's guidance:

- ★ *Solitude* and *reflection* are essential for my inward journey, but I also need *others* to help me walk through the fearsome tunnels of darkness.

- ★ In the seasons of my inner life, Sophia's presence can soften the anguish or isolation of the darkness, but she will not take it away from me. The darkness is necessary for my *growth*.

- ★ My fears and anxieties can quietly, or noisily, tend to take over my decisions and my choices if there is no *awareness* of them, sapping me of my energy for lifegiving experiences.

- ★ If I stay in the *darkness* long enough, my eyes become more accustomed to the dark, and I begin to see things of *beauty* and *freedom* that I never knew were present.

NOTE: At the end of each chapter you will find questions and suggestions that invite you into your own deep space where Sophia lives. These questions/suggestions are offered as a means of integrating the chapter's topic into your own life.

Sometimes you will find suggestions for journaling, and at other times you may be asked to create a mandala. Both are ancient forms of paying attention to what is happening inside yourself. You may want to refer to the artist's thoughts to guide you in making mandalas (see page xii).

Keeping a journal may also help you discover the inside story of who you are and who you are becoming. By writing down your feelings, ideas and insights, reflections, poems, songs, dreams, dialogues, prayers, quotes from your reading, drawings, or sketches, you become more aware of your inner life.

The keeping of a journal requires only a willingness to listen to your deepest self, to take time to record what is happening to you and to reflect periodically and observe the connections, growth, and struggles within.

If you have never kept a journal, begin by finding a notebook that feels comfortable to you — a simple three-ringed notebook or sketchbook or a special hardcover book.

Plan for a period of time when you can listen quietly to your inner being and be open and real with your recording. Pause to relax and be as much at peace as you can. Let the journal be your companion to truth and ongoing revelation about your true self.

Keeping your journal in a safe place where only you will have access to it will help you to record your true self. You may choose not to use your journal every day. The vital thing is to take time often to listen, to pay attention to your inner growing. There is a beautiful world inside of you, and a journal is one way to discover it.

Meeting Sophia

1. Take time with the stars. Sit under them. Walk with them. Let yourself dance with them. Be with these friends of the universe and let them speak to you of the journey in your heart.

2. Reflect upon the Star in your heart.
Relax your body/mind/spirit. See yourself in a place of beauty, somewhere away from the city. Use your senses to become a part of your environment. Notice how the air smells, what you hear. Sit down and feel the earth or sand or rock or .... Be attentive to all that you can see around you.

Dusk slowly comes to the place where you are sitting. Be with the sunset, the fading light, the darkness as it quietly descends upon you. See yourself sitting now in the darkness. Look up and see that the first star of the evening has come. Continue to look and see how the sky gradually fills with a brilliant star-filled expanse. Everywhere you look there are stars sparkling and glowing.

Focus on one star. See it slowly fall from the sky. It glides toward you in a welcoming way. It comes closer. Quietly, tenderly, it falls into your heart. It does so with great ease and comfort. It does not burn or harm. It only glows with peaceful light. See the star shining there for you. Rest in peace with the star. Speak to the star. Let the star speak to you. Continue to be with the star until you are both silent again. Gradually return to the daylight.

Take some time to write or draw or paint your response to this meeting of the Star in your heart. You might also consider using clay to complete this experience of the Star within you. Let the clay speak of the Star falling into your heart.

3. Reflect on your own wisdoms regarding the Star in your heart. How have you experienced darkness? What do you know of Sophia's presence in your darkness? What do you believe about your life's journey of darkness and light? Write these discovered wisdoms in your journal.

4. Ponder the mandala at the beginning of this chapter. Let yourself enter into this sacred image. After this "entering in," write a prayer to Sophia. Try drawing a mandala, a sacred circle. Fill it with symbols or words that describe the light and the dark within you.

CHAPTER TWO
FAR-SEEING EYES

She is so Pure,
She Pervades
and Permeates All Things.

WISDOM 7:24

All is quiet on the mountain
this late March morning.
Forsythia cry out their colors
while the mist still enfolds them.
The lake has nary a ripple
and the trees stand silently.
Only bird songs break the bonds
of the tranquil breath of dawn.

Inside of me it is also quiet.
No forsythia are blooming there,
but I feel the aura of stillness
and the beauty of calm waters.
It has been so long since silence
rested her wings in my heart.

The earth has gathered me in her arms,
rocking all my weariness to sleep.
Months of running and stumbling
are lain down beside the wooded path;
I lift only beauty of the present moment,
and when I place it in my heart
all my life looks differently to me.

— Joyce Rupp

Have you ever risked doing something that might possibly turn out to be a real disaster? I did when I gave a seminar on appreciating the beauty of life. I decided to ask each of the participants to take one section of orange, one small piece of apple, one strawberry, and one grape. I then invited them to take at least ten minutes to eat these four items. It was a crazy suggestion to people who usually finish a complete fast food meal in that same amount of time. But they did eat slowly. They relished the taste of each item, enjoying the colors, the feel, the shape, the smell of each before they popped the delicious bits of food into their mouths, one at a time. Afterward I drew them into a "Sophia moment": I asked them to be very still and to reflect on this experience, to see if there was a deeper meaning in it for them. Wonderful insights came forth. One person recognized how hastily she lived life and how she failed to relish and appreciate the food of her relationships, oftentimes barely noticing the goodness of her loved ones. Another saw a connection with his spiritual journey in that he, like the orange, needed to be "peeled" or to let go of some of his outer defenses before he could be nourishing and lifegiving for others. I so enjoyed their discoveries as they saw with deeper eyes that day. They confirmed my belief that if we go inward we can oftentimes see more clearly what is on the outside of our life.

But not all made these connections. As I was walking down the hall after the seminar, I heard someone from the group say to another, "I don't care what she says, a grape is a grape!" I laughed. But I also thought about what keeps some people from seeing more deeply into life. I think that a good part of the reason is simply that they have not developed their intuitive gifts and have not given themselves to the reflective process, a process that Sophia delights in with us. Sophia is the one with far-seeing eyes par excellence. She knows, she perceives, she "sees" far beyond the surface of things and the events of the present moment. "She is an initiate in the mysteries of God's knowledge" (Wisdom 8:4). It is a deep seeing that bonds her with all of life. She perceives the meaning in it. She senses the beauty that is there. Thus it is that Sophia leads me to what is unknown or invisible, to what is "far-seeing." When Sophia takes me inward, I go to the dwelling place of God. It is her light that lets me see far beneath the surface of life. When I connect this inner seeing with my outer seeing, my world takes on a different meaning for me.

14

I have long yearned to be a far-seeing person. Sometimes this yearning has been granted to me, although I am often one of those who fall into bed at night with no inner vision, hurrying through the day and missing the inner connections. But when the far-seeing moments come, they are a wondrous gift. I often find these moments recorded in my journal. Life moves so fast that I can easily forget they have happened to me unless I take time to record them. When I go back and read my journal, I am astounded at how much Sophia has blessed me.

One far-seeing moment was that of a very foggy morning when I arose to greet the God of dawn. The retreat center where I was staying had a small pond nearby that was surrounded by scotch pines. As I awoke I felt called by Sophia to go and sit on the white swing near the pond, to simply be present to the mystery before me.

As I sat there, enveloped by the wet world, the mist rose wonderfully from the pond. At times it lifted so high that the trees were clearly reflected in the water's eye. Then their images would quickly disappear with another big breath of misty air covering the pond. I felt myself becoming one with all that was there, one with the mist rising and moving, coming and going, one with the ducks preening and chewing, one with the mourning doves murmuring and cooing. I was serenely connected to the whole scene. The air over the pond cleared one more time, and the pines were again etched on the face of the water. Tears came to my eyes as I recognized my own story there, a midlife one of losing my dreams and finding them again, over and over, an alternating series of blurred vision and vibrant clarity much like the image of the trees in the misty pond. I felt greatly comforted by the pond that morning. It assured me that my inner journey was a natural part of my adult growth.

Another such experience happened to me as I went for a walk one February morning in early dawn. It was a cold wintry Midwest day, and a quiet snow was falling. There was just enough white on the ground that I could see my footprints very clearly as I stopped to relish the beauty of the snowfall. I continued my walk among the gentle snowflakes and then turned around to come home. As I approached the place where I had stopped earlier, I saw that in less than thirty minutes my footprints had disappeared, completely covered by the newly fallen snow. Something inside of me was astounded by this fact. I hurried on home and prepared for work.

As I went through the day, I kept finding the image of my "erased footprints" in my mind. That evening Sophia called to me to not let that event go without some reflection, so I sat down to be with the footprints. Then it came to me so clearly. How very quickly my life will be gone. I think of my life as vital and significant, yet I am so small and so insignificant in such a vast world. I saw how fleeting life is and how much I do treasure the gift of it. It was humbling to recognize this. The words of Psalm 90 came to me: "Teach us to count how few days we have and so gain wisdom of heart" (Psalm 90:12). Again, this gift of Sophia, this far-seeing moment, gave me a vision to keep in my heart forever, a vision to influence the way I walk through my days.

Ira Progoff, psychotherapist and professor, has described the inner self as a well. He says that as we go down into the well of our self that the stream that feeds each well feeds all the wells. This stream is the unconscious part of our self.[5] I think of the stream feeding all the wells in another way, too. I see it as the energy of the Divine in each of us, connecting us to all of life. I am interconnected to all others because of this stream that runs deep within my spirit. In a mysterious way that I cannot understand, God's loving energy fills the earth and bonds me to all who live. Likewise, I am bound and interconnected to all creatures and elements of the earth because I, too, am made of matter and energy as they are. A simple and beautiful example of this is the process of plants giving off oxygen for my body, and my body giving off carbon dioxide so plants can live.

When I see myself and the world in this way, life takes on a sacred quality. Life is already sacred in itself. The native Americans have seen this for many ages. The beauty of the holy is there, but it takes far-seeing eyes to know it, to sense the energy and the dynamism that weave the universe together.

Elizabeth Dodson Gray's works have been a special awakening for me. She writes that our culture has been obsessed with "ranking diversity." We are always deciding who and what is better or more superior. She constantly urges her readers to give up the ranking system and to see that we live in a "system that is highly inter-related." We are not separate from the rest of life. Rather, we live within that life system and are closely connected to it.[6] Sadly, I realize that for many years I have thought of humans as dominating the earth, as having a superior power over everything else that exists. Gradually I began looking in a new way, seeing how each part of life has beauty in itself and is necessary for the whole of existence. Instead of seeing myself and other humans as "better" than an acorn, a spider, a piece of driftwood, or other creatures and elements, I recognized that I am "different" from these other parts of life. I now look much more kindly upon all of the earth.

Letting go of the "better than" approach to life has also influenced my relationship with people. It has helped me to approach persons from other cultures, races, ideas, and philosophies with greater openness and reverence. I am more able to see that all are truly my sisters and brothers. I am united with them. Matter and energy connect us all. There is a vital bond that unites us. If I ignore this or try to dominate others, I know that the bond will be weakened or broken. Because of this unity, who I am and what I do greatly affects all of creation.

This connectedness with the universe is described by Thomas Merton as "the mysterious cosmic dance."[7] It is the vibrant energy of life that surges through us and through everything that exists. I have known the cosmic dance in so many ways: the sound of laughter in a delighted child's voice, the colorful traces of many types of rock found in a small stone in the mountains, the love shining in the eyes of a friend, the smell of rain on a hot summer day, the speckles on a sparrow's breast, the ocean's strong lapping of ebb and flow, the first bird song of the day, a hot air balloon rising wondrously in the blue sky, the feel of a pine cone, the taste of freshly baked bread.

This kinship and bonding with creation is reflected in Jessica Powers' poem "Ledge of Light":

> God is a thousand acres to me now
> of high sweet-smelling April and the flow
> of windy light across a high plateau.[8]

She saw something more than just the month of April and all its beauty. Jessica Powers had entered into the cosmic dance when her far-seeing eyes glimpsed the connections there between the beauty of April and her sense of God's presence.

The story of the Visitation in the Christian scriptures is a marvelous event of the cosmic dance or the leap of life that can occur in our connectedness. Two women greet one another in joy, care, love. As they embrace, life leaps in Elizabeth. The sound of Mary's voice creates a great bonding between them:

> Now as soon as Elizabeth heard Mary's greeting, the child leaped in her womb and Elizabeth was filled with the Holy Spirit. She gave a loud cry and said, " ... from the moment your greeting reached my ears, the child in my womb leaped for joy." (Luke 1:39-45)

The child dancing in this woman's womb is symbolic of the dance within each person's heart and within all the universe. When two spirits meet and are connected in tenderness, appreciation, or compassion, the Holy leaps in life from one heart to another in a wonderful cosmic leap. We feel this leap, perhaps for just a moment, as Elizabeth did, but we forever "know" this moment.

When I greet another person or any element of the universe with hospitality — that is, with welcome and acceptance, with wonder and awe — I am bonded. I connect ... and the dance goes on! It may be the sunset that fills the sky while I am caught on the freeway; it may be the first sight and touch of a baby kitten; or it may be picking up a broken limb of an elm tree in the backyard. Far-seeing moments can be very simple and ordinary, but they have a way of connecting me to the essence of life.

Earth things greet me, call to me, welcome me. Rocks, stones, stars, inanimate objects, all carry some kind of greeting. How can a stone speak to me? It does so simply by what it is. I have a wonderful, flat, rounded stone tossed up by the ocean on the north shore of Oahu. Each time I hold this porous, sand-torn stone, I feel a oneness with the ocean, with the Creator, with all of life. This simple element carried in the ocean, for perhaps many years, greets me with a profound sense of history. Something in me stirs in gratitude and awe whenever I look upon it.

Trees also have a special way of connecting me to the cosmic dance. The leap of life fills my spirit when I spend time with them. I sense a dynamic energy there waiting to be received by my spirit. One morning when I was attending a seminar in Louisville, I walked by a pine tree whose arms were filled with fresh spring growth. The lime-green shoots were a beauty to behold. Sophia drew me to a stop. I stood there with the pine tree, opened my hands, and asked to receive the energy and the beauty of that life-filled tree. As I walked through the rest of the day, I felt a quiet energy radiating in me because of that momentary pause on my morning walk.

I have also known this deep bonding with life in the bruised and battered elements of the universe. I have hurt with the scarred faces of the land worn out with neglect or overuse. I have felt pain to see strong, old oak trees ripped out for new shopping malls; to walk along streams cluttered with debris and trash; to see the city air filled with smog and harsh pollutants.

The ache in me goes deep when faces of starving children and bodies of people in war-torn countries stare at me from the newspaper or the evening news. Because I see my connectedness with all of life, I weep for the people of the world who are in pain. And I weep for the elements of the universe because we are all webbed together in this cosmic dance.

This sense of pain comes through far-seeing moments when I have recognized this interweaving of everyone and everything. It draws me to compassion. There is a calling to my heart to be united with all who are suffering. I have found that it is oftentimes the ones who have suffered greatly who most clearly sense this bond with others who hurt. When they move beyond their own pain, they find themselves in a unique communion or bondedness with other hurting ones of the earth. Etty Hillesum is one such person. In her late twenties she faced the certitude of the camps of the Holocaust and extermination. She saw this coming and faced it bravely. Her diaries are filled with compassion and care for all the earth. She became more and more united with everyone as she came nearer to her own time of death. Etty wrote:

> One day I would love to travel all the world, oh God. I feel drawn right across all frontiers and feel a bond with all your warring creatures.[9]
> ... through suffering I have learned that we must share our love with all creation.[10]

What does all of this have to do with you and me as we try to see beyond the pile of dishes in the kitchen or get through the stacks of papers on our desks? I think the essence of far-seeing eyes is that this treasure is available to every person in whatever circumstance of life. Sophia yearns to share this vision with us. "Sophia moments" are waiting for us. They happen when we, for just a brief time, have a clarity of vision about who we are and how life is. When this happens there is a newly opened freedom in the depths of ourselves. It is like a clearing in the forest, or a traffic jam finally moving, or a headache suddenly gone. People of far-seeing eyes live with much more joy and wonder because they have looked beyond the surface of life and have found sustaining, hopeful, enduring truths that nudge them on to hope.

★

Here are some of the wisdoms to which Sophia is leading me in my moments of far-seeing eyes:

★ When I stop the hurry in my life, pause for leisure and *be-ing time*, I can much more easily join in Sophia's dance of life.

★ Sophia draws me to look upon all of life with the vision that it is sacred, helping me to *reverence* and to cherish all people, creatures and elements of the universe.

★ My *external senses*, as well as my internal ones, such as intuition and emotion, facilitate the process of joining my outer world with my inner world, giving me deeper vision and clarity of life.

★ I will always be incomplete when I lack *compassion*, which is the love born out of reverence and of suffering.

Meeting Sophia

1. Reflect on some of your far-seeing moments. When did they happen? What are some of the wisdoms that they have given to you?

2. Pick up the daily newspaper. Read the front page. How connected and bonded in compassion are you to the people and situations that you find there?

3. Select several of your far-seeing moments. Note how your senses helped you to come to deeper truth at those times. Choose to spend some quiet time with each of your five external senses. One day, be aware of your gift of hearing; another day, your gift of sight, etc. You might also choose to write a dialogue with the sense of which you are least aware. What does this sense "say" to you?

4. Reflect on Sophia "at play" everywhere.
Envision the cosmic dance going on in you and in all creation. Image and sense your participation in this wonderful dance. Take paints or colors and draw the cosmic dance within you and within all the universe.
   You might conclude this imaging with dancing. Play some of your favorite music or go outdoors and dance with the earth.

5. Go for a walk — slowly — or sit upon the ground. Be very attentive to the earth and to your surroundings. Find something of the earth and befriend it (a leaf, a weed, a flower, a stone . . .). Look upon it long. What connectedness is there between you and the earth? What does your earth gift tell you of your life?

6. Read Luke 1:39–45. How does this leap of life happen for you when you are with others?

CHAPTER THREE
THE ENCHANTED FOREST

She Will Give . . .
the Bread of Understanding to Eat,
and the Water of Wisdom to Drink.

ECCLESIASTICUS 15:3

Have you ever felt love
deep and strong in you
like a glass of good red wine?
And then this love
falls out of your heart
breaking into so many pieces?

The ache is dull yet deep;
when you look inside
to where the love was
you see this empty spot;
you feel its all-gone-ness.

I've felt that way before.
All the good warmth in me
shattered by other's harshness.
Love fell out of me
before I could catch it,
and then I ever so slowly
kicked at the pieces around me
wondering if I cared enough
to stoop low, to bend down,
to begin to pick them up.

O love, how fragile you are
and sometimes so deceptive
in your supposed strength.
O love, how fickle you are
to leap out of my heart
at the sound of pettiness.
O love, did I ever have you
or was it just delusion
and so much of a wishing well?

— Joyce Rupp

"Why don't you grow up?" This question was asked of me by my elders when I was young. It happened when I was being my worst self, either fighting with my brothers and sisters or else behaving in a way that was totally unacceptable to the adults who were present. Unconsciously, I probably associated "growing up" with a magical stage of adulthood where I could stop growing, an age where I would know just what to do and would be just who I was supposed to be. I would have all the right answers to life's problems. I think that I was in my early thirties before I realized that I would always be "growing up," that I would always be discovering more of who I am, that I would always be in the process of maturing, ripening, and becoming whole. When I first came to this realization I was terribly discouraged, but now I find joy in this reality and look forward to the possibilities of undreamed growth. I find this exciting and enriching, although this does not mean that I am always so enthused about the pain that usually accompanies the growth.

Sophia has given me much hope and courage in my process of growing up. It is her "bread of understanding" and her "water of wisdom" that continue to nourish and to strengthen me as I search for and accept the person I am becoming. I have grown in my trust of her presence. Each time I approach another step in growing up, I realize that it is Sophia's movement in my spirit that leads me to greater understanding and wisdom. I see Sophia as an ever-present guide who is always ready to help me to continue to grow up.

As a child growing into adulthood, I gradually developed a number of understandings or beliefs about life. They were my dreams, my goals, my vision of life, my ideas about how life is or ought to be. These beliefs came to me from my parents, teachers, friends, religion, life experiences, books, and numerous other influences. I stored up these beliefs in my heart like some kind of enchanted forest, a Camelot of values and ideals. Whenever I went into that forest of beliefs, I felt that life was good, right, and true. All my beliefs in my enchanted forest seemed so real. When life challenged me, I would go to that forest and look for one of my deep and strong truths so that I could feel comfortable, safe, and secure.

I have been able to discover some of my enchanted forest beliefs by listening to myself, my own messages of "I'll always ... I should ... I must ... I have to ... I can't ... I won't ... They should ... They must ..."

Some of my enchanted forest messages that I have discovered in my own life or in the life of others are:

"I can overcome anything. Defeat and failure do not need to be a part of my life."

"Our family has very close ties. We will never let material possessions like inheritances alienate us or separate us."

"If I have good friends (or a good marriage or a good community ...), I will never have to be lonely."

"My friends will always stand by me."

"Our love will last forever."

"If I just work hard enough and get enough education, it will be easy for me to get a good job."

"God will grant positive answers to my prayers if I pray long enough or learn how to pray in the 'right way'."

"My parents can do no wrong."

"I will have the perfect marriage or the perfect children or the perfect ..."

"Our children will develop into responsible adults because we have tried so hard to give them our values."

"The church is always right."

"I won't age or get worn out or develop illnesses."

"My faith is strong and enduring. I won't ever need to question the existence of God."

"If I am kind to others they will be kind to me."

27

"Someday I am going to find a real balance in my life between work and play, between action and contemplation."

One of my biggest "growing up" experiences has been that of "disenchantment": having to go to my enchanted forest of beliefs and discover that what gave me such comfort or sense of direction no longer does so for me. "Growing up" has been, and is, the process of discovering which of my beliefs is steadfast and which needs to be changed, adapted, or possibly even discarded entirely. Often when I experience disenchantment I feel wounded, empty, maybe even betrayed by someone or betrayed by my own truths, which I thought were so accurate and so right for me. Sometimes it is just a momentary feeling of confusion or discouragement, and sometimes the hurt lasts for a long, long time.

This disenchantment is especially essential to the midlife process. It is here that we begin to recognize that what worked for us at one time in our life just does not do so any longer because we are not the same persons that we were in our younger years.

Because of our life experiences we are forced to face the challenge of our enchanted forests. I remember so well the pain of this for a participant in one of my midlife classes. There was such anguish in her eyes and disillusionment in her voice as she spoke with the group. She was a woman in her early forties and was sharing a professional struggle she had recently faced. She described how one of the people with whom she worked had been out to get her, had tried to destroy her reputation with ugly rumors and untruths. As this hurting woman told her story, she said sadly, "I've always trusted people. I never thought that someone I worked with would deliberately try to ruin my life. Are people really that cruel? I don't think I can ever trust anyone again." As she spoke I realized that one of her beliefs had been shattered. Her enchanted world of trusting others had been challenged. Now she would have to learn to trust again and to adjust her understanding of how people might respond to her.

William Bridges writes about disenchantment in his book *Transitions*. He points out that disenchantment is a natural part of endings or significant transitions. It is difficult, at first, to see any meaning in the disenchantment experience. It hurts too much.

> But later it is important to reflect on these things, for with realities as with identities and connections, the old must be cleared away before the new can grow. The mind is a vessel that must be emptied if new wine is to be put in.[11]

It is in this reflection time that I see Sophia being an essential helper to me, bringing light and encouragement. For she helps me to see that all of this is essential if I am to continue growing. Sophia stands by me and assures me that the pain is worth the "new wine" that is to come. Judith Viorst describes the process this way:

> The road to human development is paved with renunciation. Throughout our life we grow by giving up. We give up some of our deepest attachments to others. We give up certain cherished parts of ourselves. We must confront, in the dreams we dream, as well as in our intimate relationships, all that we never will have and never will be.[12]

I have learned much from others and how they have struggled with the pain of disenchantment. I recall my father's angry outburst when he learned that my sister would be married in a church that was not of our religion. He felt wounded and hurt. He was determined not to attend. But with time and reflection (and some good talks with my mother), he did take part in the ceremony. Later on he developed a close friendship with my sister's husband. But before that time it was a hard moment of disenchantment for my father because he had believed and hoped that all his children would pursue his own religious beliefs. He had to let go of that belief. When I saw him at the wedding, I was proud of his decision and knew that it took great courage for him to act as he did.

My mother has also been a witness for me in how to walk into the enchanted forest and make necessary changes. She has strong, deep tenets of faith, yet is able to adapt with the times. She has opened her heart and home to those who have chosen ways that she never would have in her youth. Children and grandchildren with values and lifestyles that are very different from her own have been a challenge to her enchanted forest. Sometimes the disenchantment moments have brought their share of tears and times of sadness. But she is a woman of reflection, and her hospitable spirit is a rich sign of her own adaptation or letting go of past beliefs in order to grow.

My own disenchantments often happen at the most unusual times or places. One day as I drove on the freeway, I was deep in thought with Sophia, tumbling around a painful situation. I was feeling very wounded by a coworker, someone I had trusted and had tried to help when she was new on our staff. I had given my time and energy to help her get acquainted and situated in her new position. I felt open and welcoming toward this colleague. But I discovered as the year went on that she did not feel the same way about me. As I pondered this hurt, a startling revelation came to me: No matter how open I try to be, no matter how hard I work at relating well with others, I will always have some enemies. I realized in a flash of insight that, because of who I am and the way life is, not everyone is going to approach me with welcome. I did not like this bit of truth. It challenged my belief that I could get along with everyone.

Then I began to see the value of having a few enemies. I actually found myself thanking God for them because I realized how much they had taught me about the parts of myself that I never wanted to look at: my own weaknesses that so easily pop up when I have to relate with those who are at odds with me. Thus, my enemies actually lead me to see parts of myself that I can so easily tend to hide.

Another painful disenchantment time for me was when I came to terms with the fact that my religious community is made up of individuals who are just as human as everyone else in the world. This was an extended time of disenchantment for me. I had such strong ideals and beliefs when I first joined my community, and I felt sure that it was possible for this group to be a model group of loving, dynamic women who lived the Gospel values fully. What a rude awakening it was when I realized that there were personality clashes, differing views of theology and philosophies of life, power struggles and emotional weaknesses that sometimes forced us apart rather than drew us together. Eventually I saw, to my great chagrin, that I, too, had a great many flaws that contributed to the flawed condition of the whole. Gradually I was able to change my focus from the incompleteness of the community to the many positive aspects that were there. As we struggled through renewal, I came to appreciate much more keenly the deep commitment and genuine desire for God that grew in the hearts of so many of my sisters in the community. In this disenchantment era I went to my forest of beliefs and adapted my expectations of my community members and of our leadership teams. Today I have a much more realistic and healthy outlook on how we live religious life.

This same thing happens to many of my married friends. They think they will have the perfect marriage and then they begin to see the flaws in one another. It takes a long time to adapt expectations and to learn to love unconditionally while experiencing one another's unfinishedness.

I am still going back often to my enchanted forest of beliefs. I continue to ask Sophia to keep me open and free. Probably the most difficult disenchantment for me has been that of my membership in the Roman Catholic Church. The male-dominated structures and laws of this system tear at my vision of a church in which I believe all ought to be given respect and accepted with their gifts and talents. One of my deep beliefs has been that the church is one place where injustice should never happen. But I have had to change this belief as I have seen women being refused ordination, married priests ostracized, and many power struggles turn into hierarchical dictatorships. I have adjusted and adapted, and now I believe that injustice should not happen in the church, but it does because the church is human. However, this fact is still wounding to me. Disenchantment is painful, and adjustment can be long and hard.

Sometimes there are beliefs in our enchanted forest that need to endure. One of mine that I want to continue is my belief in the right of justice for every person. My struggle with injustice in the church has deepened this belief in me rather than weakened or adapted it. I know that I need to change my expectations of the church, but I also know that I must keep alive my vision of justice for all. I trust that Sophia will guide me in this.

When I look at my own disenchantments and those of others, I see that "expectations" often get in the way of growth. My expectations of self, others, life, church, even God, can be unreal or unhealthy. I end up putting so much energy into trying to have my expectations met that I actually harm myself by using so much inner energy and losing my view on the larger picture of life.

When disenchantment happens, it is a real challenge to look at life positively. Sometimes this takes a while, and I must simply be patient with the time it takes to recover, to adjust, to "try on" an adapted version of my belief, or to decide to discard the whole thing. It is a time to stay very close to Sophia in prayer and reflection. It is a time to trust that Sophia will lead the way into the enchanted forest and also to trust that she will help me to find the way back out of it, wiser and healthier in what I believe to be true about life.

★

Here are some of the wisdoms that Sophia is giving to me as I walk into and struggle with my enchanted forest:

★ Although I will continually find areas in my life and my beliefs that are incomplete, *I am still "okay"* now. I simply have much yet to discover about who I am.

★ Growing up does not mean that I cast away all of my hopes and dreams, but it does call me to *look at those beliefs* carefully, seeing how open I am to the possibility of adapting or changing them.

★ Sophia will guide me and nurture me as I go into my enchanted forest, helping me to know what *beliefs* I need *to discard* and which ones I need *to keep.*

★ *Others* who have gone through times of disenchantment can be a source of courage and strength for me. It is also *helpful* for me to tell my story to others, for in saying it I often hear for the first time where I am going on my inner journey.

Meeting Sophia

1. Go into your own enchanted forest. Reflect on your basic beliefs about life, self, God, others. List these.
   - Which ones have endured for you?
   - Which ones have you adapted?
   - Which ones have you discarded?
   - Which ones have you added?

2. Draw an enchanted forest. Make a path leading into the forest. On this path, list feelings you have when you walk into this forest in times of disenchantment. Make a path leading out of the forest. On this path, list the feelings you have when you walk out of the forest with new or adapted beliefs.

3. Ask others to tell you the story of their disenchantments.

4. Draw a mandala of your enchanted forest when you were ten years old. Then draw a mandala of your enchanted forest now.

5. If someone asked you what kinds of disenchantment you have experienced, what would you say? What suggestions would you have for someone who is going through a difficult time of disenchantment?

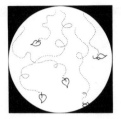

CHAPTER FOUR
LEAF BY LEAF BY LEAF

. . . Knowing She Would be My Counselor in Prosperity,
My Comfort in Cares and Sorrows

WISDOM 8:9

Leaf by leaf by leaf
they tumble and fall:
all my haggard hurts.

like a cottonwood tree
ever so slowly letting go,
so the heartache of my heart.

there goes a bit of sadness,
now a leaf of anger flies;
then it's the dropping of self-pity.

the leaf of unforgiveness
takes forever to fall,
almost as long as non-trusting.

leaf by leaf by leaf
they fall from my heart,
like a tree in its own time.

old wounds don't heal quickly,
they drop in despairing slowness,
never looking at the clock.

it seems a forever process,
this healing of the hurt,
and I am none too patient.

but a quiet day finally comes
when the old tree with no leaves,
is decidedly ready for the new.

and in my waiting heart,
the branches with no leaves
have just a hint of green.

— Joyce Rupp

"You don't know exactly when resentment leaves you. It happens gradually," she said. "One day you just wake up and you know you are not carrying resentment around in you anymore." The participants in the midlife seminar listened intently as this woman shared her struggle of personal growth with them. Then they added their own stories to the wisdom of how slowly healing happens.

I have found this gradual process to be very true in my own life as well. Several years ago when I was on an extended retreat, I was very aware of Sophia as my companion to the dark places. I felt her urging me to take a closer look at some areas of my life that needed healing. I remembered the assurances of the author of Proverbs: ". . . she will keep you safe . . . she will watch over you" (Proverbs 4:6). This remembrance and promise of Sophia's presence gave me the courage to gather up some of my old wounds. As I remembered them, I felt very discouraged. The feelings of anger and unforgiveness came back strongly, jabbing me with their sharp edges. I had hoped they would have long been gone but, no, there they were, persistent in their negative attacks on my inner peace.

As I prayed about these memories and the feelings that accompanied them, I looked up at a nearby tree. It was a sturdy, tall cottonwood. The season was early autumn, and the tree was just beginning to lose its leaves. I sat there entwined in the leaf-letting process. One by one the golden leaves twirled to the earth. I watched them sail down for several hours. Then the wisdom of the event came to me: The tree would not lose all its leaves in one day. And I would not be healed of my hurt in one chunk of time either. My hurts would leave me gradually. I could not hurry them away.

Weeks earlier I had written in my journal:

Anger comes and goes these days, as swift as a minute, as slow as a week. It rages and fumes in me, takes me for long memory walks where blood and guts are seen. Then anger goes away, leaves me all alone, pretending to be dissolved and maybe even dead. But let someone pronounce against

38

me and I am off again to mutter life's inequities, with anger urging me on to atrocities of the heart. Is there a gentle voice in me that weeps for all this terror that rises up in me? When will the flames of anger finally die out? When will I be at peace? When will I be at home with my true self again?

I so wanted to have the anger and the harsh feelings quickly leave me. This urge to have immediate healing is, of course, a product of the culture in which I live, which wants instant everything. If I can take a pill to get rid of my headache right away, why can't I do that to the pains inside of me, too? It is hard to picture a wound of the psyche or the inner self in the way that I would see a physical wound on my body. Yet, they are very similar in that they both need time to heal — and they both must heal from the inside out, not just on the surface, which can heal more quickly. Hurried healing or surface healing will never do. There will be festering inside, and eventually the poison of the wound will ooze out in misdirected emotions.

Sometimes, too, it may seem that the healing really is completed over an extended period of time and then, unexpectedly, a strong painful feeling surfaces from the experience of long ago. A woman who was on retreat was very upset when she found herself filled with grief for her mother who had died eight years earlier. She felt that she had really grieved her mother's death and was at peace with it. Yet, there she was, filled with deep sadness again. What was going on? She spoke about being out of the country at the time of her mother's death. When she had agreed to travel for her work, her mother was aging but not seriously ill. But within a week after her departure overseas, her mother died. She was unable to return for the funeral, but when she did return she relived the death and funeral through the stories and comments of her brothers and sisters. She felt that she had grieved sufficiently in the years that followed, that she had truly let go of her mother. Then, why the tears that would not stop coming? As she searched for the cause of her pain, she saw that she had never forgiven herself for the decision to be so far away. Although it was not her fault, she felt that she had made a poor decision. She needed to forgive herself for it. As she did so during the retreat time, another part of her deep woundedness over her mother's death was healed. Another leaf fell from her tree of hurt.

I have found that breaches and breaks in relationships are the hardest wounds to heal. They go so deep and seem to take much longer than physical deaths of loved ones, serious illnesses, job losses, or many other negatives in life. When there are betrayals, rejections, false judgments, angry accusations, deadly jealousies, or power struggles, the pain wedges itself in the human heart like an ax ripping through green wood. It may take many years before that giant gouge in the heart is mended.

Another reason that healing takes such a long time is the extent of the damage that the wound has caused. Who did the wounding and how vulnerable we were at the time makes a difference. The deeper the wounding, the longer the healing time.

Many childhood hurts are deep because we are so tender and so fully trusting. These hurts are carried into adult years because they are repressed or never acknowledged. Particularly in the midlife years, these painful memories surface and need to be dealt with in order to have genuine peace and greater wholeness. Verbal, physical, or sexual abuse cause major wounds in childhood that often take years to heal. Nicknames, sibling rivalries, parents who did not know how to parent, teachers who unknowingly blamed and maimed, also cause deep hurts that are remembered in later life and need to be resolved. Many times the memory of one wound leads to the discovery of another one. The leaves on the tree seem never to stop falling. It can become very discouraging. Giving oneself to the journey of healing, and accepting the fact that it may take a long time, is essential for the process. Bad memories do not just go away once we are aware of them. But by our working through them, they can lose their power over us and their strong influence on the way that we live our lives. Personal therapy and support groups are a helpful means to gain courage for the extended time of healing.

Sometimes healing takes a long time because of the way we learned to ignore our hurts, not recognizing how extensive they are. When one of my friends was a small child, she was playing with some of the neighborhood children in an old abandoned garage near their home. As they began to chase each other, she slipped and hit her head on a sharp edge of iron. She put her hand on the back of her head, saw that it was full of blood, and screamed in terror. As she ran for home her father met her, looked at her, and said, "Stop that bawling! It's not that bad. You shouldn't have been playing in there anyway." No sympathy. No comfort. No recognition of her fear of how badly she was hurt. From this one experience she grew into adulthood believing three things about her deep wounds: (a) ignore them, (b) they don't hurt nearly as much as you think they do, (c) it's your fault that you hurt so much. Consequently, she tended to ignore her inner pain and to stuff her feelings far away inside of herself, thinking that she should not hurt as much as she did.

Healing will not happen unless our feelings are recognized and owned as ours. We must believe that we are of enough value to take the time to listen to these feelings. Feelings such as anger, jealousy, and hatred are especially hard to claim because they have been named by the church as "sins." Yet, they are natural human emotions and never sinful unless we choose to use these feelings against others or ourselves. Our healing is impeded when we do not acknowledge our negative feelings. Sometimes others will not allow us to own these feelings. At a seminar for recently divorced, many of the divorcees spoke of how their families and friends did not want to hear their negative feelings. One woman said that she had always come across as a strong person who could handle almost everything in life. She hesitated to tell people how she really felt when she was down and depressed. One day she finally shared her hostile, angry feelings with a good friend. He said, "Oh, come on, you're a strong cookie." She looked at him and said, "Oh, yeah? Well, even strong cookies crumble sometimes." When she was able to say that to her friend, another leaf fell from her tree and she took a big step toward healing.

I have learned from my own life that holding onto negative feelings can also extend the healing process unnecessarily. I heard a wise

41

saying once that has helped me with this: "Negative feelings are like stray cats. The more you feed them, the more they hang around." Nursing grudges, rehashing old arguments, bathing in self-pity, or feeding the fires of anger takes a lot of lifegiving energy. How much healthier to use the inner energy toward positive things happening in our lives. This is not to deny the negative emotions or to avoid dealing with them; rather, it is to eventually move beyond them. We can not hang onto our old negatives and expect healing and new life to happen for us.

Healing takes longer when we refuse to let go of the past. If we allow our old wounds and memories to cling to us like destructive leeches, they will sap us of our lifegiving energy and drain us of hope. Letting go is as essential for growth as it is for any element in nature. If we cling to, or hang onto, our wounds out of fear, insecurity, or self-pity, the leaf-by-leaf process takes that much longer.

On a trip to Minnesota one summer, I was enthralled with the white splendor of the birch trees. I took long walks in the woods and often stopped to ponder the beautiful groves of white trees on the way. I was amazed at how their skin-like bark readily peeled off. My friend told me that the trees could not grow unless their bark continued to come off, making room for new growth. She also hastily reminded me, as I began to pull off some of the bark, that if I took the birch bark off before its time, that the tree would be wounded. The bark had to come off in the tree's own time. "How like a birch tree I am," I thought, "only I want the bark to come rolling off all at once!"

Another aspect of letting go is that it can leave one feeling very vulnerable and cautious. Lobsters shed their shells at least seven times in their first year of life. Each time they shed the shell, it allows for more growth. When they do so, they are very vulnerable to their predators. So they hide in the sand until a new shell grows to protect them.

I remember a time when I felt very lobster-ish, having finally risked leaving a work situation that had brought a lot of pain for me because of the power struggles there. I loved my work, but I could no longer tolerate the dysfunctional style of leadership that was a part of it, so I chose to change jobs. I did not realize how cautious I was at my new position until one day I was appalled to find myself mistrusting the kindness and the care of the new staff. I saw then how I was unconsciously withholding my trust. I had been hiding in the sand, afraid of being in the midst of battle again. To my great relief there were no predators there. I let go of my fear and began a wonderful new surge of energy and a giant move toward healing of the past.

Refusing to forgive others can add years to the healing of old wounds. So can the refusal to forgive ourselves. It may be "nothing" that we actually did, but it feels like "something" that we should or should not have said or done. According to our judgment, we failed the other person or situation. Whether we have actually failed miserably, or whether we just think we have, we need to make a peace treaty with ourselves and let another leaf fall from the tree. So, too, with asking others for forgiveness when we have actually failed: It is one thing to feel forgiveness for another, but the healing process can get stuck when forgiveness is not asked for.

How does Sophia enter into the leaf-by-leaf experience? I see her presence as being essential to our healing. First, Sophia gives us the strength to go through whatever is necessary for healing, whether that is the naming of feelings we would rather not have, drawing forth old memories, offering or receiving forgiveness, or being patient with the length of the healing. "She [Sophia] deploys her strength from one end of the earth to the other, ordering all things for good" (Wisdom 8:1). This strength is there within me because Sophia dwells within me. I may feel weak, inadequate, rough-edged, but I can draw on Sophia's energy to sustain me and to hold me in those long leaf-by-leaf times.

Sophia is there to give comfort to me as I face my pain, wage my inner battles, and let go of whatever is necessary for healing. Sophia understands the sorrow and the grief that wrap around my heart at times. She is a compassionate and caring presence for me. "I therefore determined to take her to share my life, knowing she would be my counsellor in prosperity, my comfort in cares and sorrow" (Wisdom 8:9).

43

Sophia also leads me to greater wisdom when I am in the leaf-by-leaf time. She helps me to see that my wounds can bless me with wisdom if I am willing to reflect upon them. Many times I am led to insights that give me courage and hope. This is Sophia at work, guiding me to greater growth.

It was in reflecting upon one of my wounds and the need for forgiveness that Sophia led me to the Genesis story of Joseph. For the first time I saw that Joseph, who is pictured as the model of forgiveness in the Hebrew scriptures, had twenty years to process his woundedness and to forgive those who had betrayed him. And even with those twenty years between him and his betrayers, he was still filled with a tremendous rush of emotion when he met them again. Scripture tells us that "when Joseph made himself known to all his brothers he wept so loudly that all the Egyptians heard" (Genesis 45:2). I thought of what deep ache must have filled Joseph's heart. His love of his brothers was deep but so was the pain of reconciliation. I found great comfort in knowing that this model of forgiveness must also have experienced the healing process in the slow falling of leaf by leaf. The pain did not just go away instantly for Joseph, either.

Finally, Sophia has been, and is, my touch of hope when I am in the healing process. So many times she has guided me to an insight or to an experience that tells me all will be well in time. One such insight was a trip to the devastated volcanic area of Mt. St. Helens. I remember vividly the hope that rose up in me when I saw the bright red flowers of the fireweed pushing their way through all the blackened volcanic earth. This image of the fireweed blooming among the rubble has become one of my symbols of healing. It tells me that, no matter how bleak the look of my heart, there will be new growth in time. It is the way of the earth, and it is the way of Sophia's dwelling in the human spirit. She guides us to hope. Because of my fireweed image, I can be more patient with the time it takes to heal. I know that eventually there will be a fresh spring leafing in my very self just as there will be new green shoots on the tree.

★

Some of the wisdoms that Sophia is offering me about healing are these:

★ As long as I am human, there will be *wounds* in my life. The deeper the wounds, the longer it will take to be healed of them.

★ I need to *be patient* with the process of inner healing. I can rely on Sophia to encourage and enable the healing to happen.

★ What I have *learned and experienced* in my youth about being hurt will make a great difference in how I approach my healing.

★ A *vision of hope* will help to carry me through the tough times of pain. Sophia can guide me to images that will gift me with hope.

Meeting Sophia

1. As you look back on your life, what have you learned about inner wounds and the healing process? How do you approach these hurts? How do you give yourself to the healing process? What do you do, or not do, with your negative feelings?

2. Make a list of some of your inner wounds, heartaches, hurts that you have experienced. Look over the list. Check the ones that have not yet been healed. Underline the ones that most need your attention.

3. Draw a tree. Label it with one of your wounds that needs to heal. Draw leaves falling off of the tree. On the falling leaves write your wounded feelings.

4. On your list of inner wounds, write next to each what you think and feel needs to be done for more healing to happen. What action might you develop that will encourage healing to take place?

5. Find someone you can trust, someone with whom you feel safe. Tell that person the story of your woundedness.

6. Draw a mandala. Fill it with the pain of one of your unhealed hurts. Draw another mandala. Fill it with the joy of a hurt that has been healed.

7. What is your vision of hope as you go through times of healing? (What is your fireweed?) Draw it or write it down and place it where you can read it or look at it often.

CHAPTER FIVE
TREASURED MEMORIES

*. . . for Memories of Me
are Sweeter than Honey.*

ECCLESIASTICUS 24:20

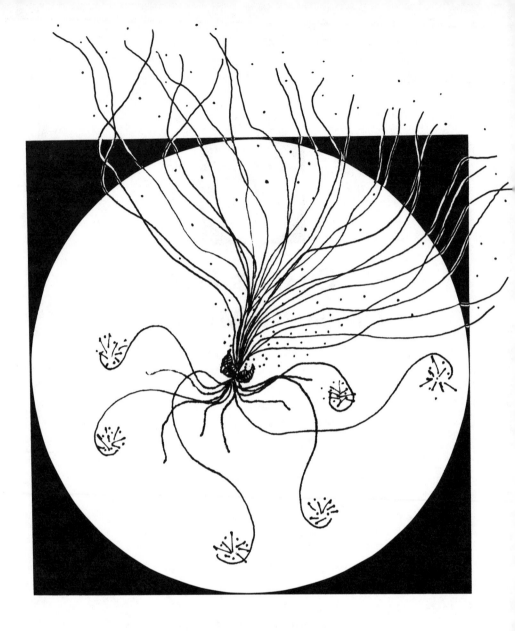

gathered together am I
from a history-held-mystery,
a bundle of memories am I.

caught from smiles and heartaches
of faces and places past cherished,
given in love from the heart of life.

from kisses and love making,
from caring and growing,
from vibrancy and vitality,
the gathered memories
of my own named person
have been gifted into existence.

surprises from seeds and secrets,
gifts from unknown voices and events;
here am I, so ordinary, so unique.
here am I, so simple, so complex.
knowing that the seed of my self
has the touch of gathered memories;
gleaned from the ages of another time,
seed and sperm seeking, making known.

a birthed bundle surprised into life,
light filling the center of a new spirit;
the blessing of eternity passed on:
urgency always to seek the face of God,
first gatherer of all good memories.

— *Joyce Rupp*

I never knew John Houseman, but I felt a strong bonding with him the day he died. A week before Thanksgiving the national news carried the story of the death of this well-respected actor and producer. John Houseman had been interviewed a month before this, and clips of the interview were televised. When asked about his illness and his dying, he said that his life was absolutely crammed full of miracles that he did not deserve — but they kept on happening to him.

Tears came to my eyes. I was deeply touched by that remark. I looked at my own life with utter amazement and gratitude as I remembered the people, the events and experiences, the insights and the surprises of spiritual growth that were a part of who I had become. As with Houseman, I felt so undeserving of it all. I never expected so much goodness to come to me.

The memory of that interview stayed with me throughout the Thanksgiving season and since then has often drawn me into gratitude and joy. In that newscast Sophia had once more befriended me. I felt it was she who had opened my being to receive those graced words of John Houseman. She took me by the hand, as she often does, and led me to renewed truth. It was a moment of blessed surprise in which I saw anew the need to live one day at a time, and to do so with deep gratitude.

The ability to remember is a gift that I can so easily take for granted. I have never thought of thanking Sophia for the gift of my neural engram, which is the memory trace in the brain, but I have often found myself filled with thanksgiving for the content of my treasured memories.

Bad memories, or memories which bring negative feelings, take away my zest for life. They are memories which, when recalled, need to be recognized and dealt with and then put aside. Treasured or cherished memories are the ones that give me energy when I recall them. They refuel my enthusiasm for life. I believe it is necessary for all of us to gather up our good, lifegiving memories and to carry them in the pockets of our hearts. Whenever we take them out and look upon them, we can be filled with hope. As we gaze upon the past goodness of our life, we can believe again in its future possibilities for us.

Gratitude is at the core of a healthy spiritual life. It helps me to recognize how cherished I am by God and to live in awareness of the generous daily miracles provided by God. I cannot be grateful without the gift of memory, without recalling or recognizing the good things of my life. Memory helps me to be aware of my Sophia moments, those times when I have been drawn to deeper truths and wisdoms. Remembering my past blessings helps me to see how deeply involved God is with my life.

Remembrances of people, places, and events are often recalled by photographs. I do not have photos of God, but I do have the scriptures, as well as my own remembered experiences of how God has been with me and for me. I have pictures in my mind and heart of my relationship with God. The purpose of remembering these is to keep the relationship alive and to strengthen it.

The Hebrew and Christian scriptures are one big photo album of God. These scriptures began with an oral tradition. Stories were told from one generation to another as people recalled how they experienced God with them. They continually retold the stories to keep this vivid memory alive. The book of Deuteronomy urges the Hebrew people, "Do not forget the things your eyes have seen, nor let them slip from your heart all the days of your life. Rather, tell them to your children and to your children's children" (Deuteronomy 4:9).

Mary of Nazareth was a woman who walked closely with Sophia. Mary reflected often on the events of her life, looking at them like photographs, pondering them, recalling what had taken place, seeing there the truths that were a part of her life. In Luke's story of Mary's giving birth to Jesus, he tells us that "as for Mary, she treasured all these things and pondered them in her heart" (Luke 2:19).

Another time Mary took her life events into memory was when she feared for her lost child and then found him in the temple, safe and at home with the teachers there. After finding Jesus, Luke tells us that "his mother stored all these things in her heart" (Luke 2:52). Mary obviously did not forget the things her eyes had seen, nor did she let them slip from her heart.

It is this remembering that is the focus of chapters ten and eleven of the Book of Wisdom in which parts of the story of the Exodus are retold. The author tells us that Sophia is the one who journeys with the people: "Wisdom delivered her servants from their ordeals . . . led by her along straight paths . . . she showed . . . the knowledge of holy things" (Wisdom 10:9-10). In these two chapters the strength and the guidance of Sophia are emphasized. Each time the story was retold, they were remembering "the marvels God has done" (Psalm 105:5).

The same thing happens in my life. The experiences of my own life with God are not written in the scriptures, but they are also significant and valuable because they, too, keep my relationship with God alive. These memories are like inner photo albums that I can take out and ponder whenever I so desire. Here are some of the treasures in my inner photo album:

> . . . moments when peace slipped surprisingly into my spirit and stayed for a while
>
> . . . wonderful relationships that surprised me with their goodness and love
>
> . . . times of truth when I got to know myself and my world better
>
> . . . messengers of Sophia who told me of her nearness by the way that they held me close and stayed with me in the tough times
>
> . . . the numerous ways my inner self has been nourished and fed by beauty, books, art, music, worship with others, and personal prayer times

... celebrative gatherings and events that increased my joy and delight in life and filled me with laughter and a sense of contentment

... challenges which led me to be more aware of the earth's needy ones

... simple moments of life when I have been touched by the beauty and goodness in others

Good memories of loved ones sustain me. They give me the courage to go on when I want to give up along the way. They connect, unite, and bond me across many miles and ages. Probably no author has expressed this more vividly and poignantly for me than Viktor Frankl when he wrote about the memory of his wife while he was a prisoner at Auschwitz. On the days when he felt he simply could not endure the horrors and the pain any longer, he would recall images of his beloved. He would remember how she smiled at him, how she looked when they had been together. As he did so, he would feel her presence, and it was as though he could reach out and touch her hand. As he communed with his beloved wife in this way, he was able to bear the insults of the guards and to endure the wretchedness of his life. The image of his beloved in his memory sustained him and brought him inner strength.[13]

My own memories of my last farewell to loved ones before they have died has been a strong connecting link with them: a dear friend's words through her raspy nose tube, "Joyce, let your heart be at peace"; the radiant smile and the dancing eyes of the cancer-stricken body of another friend as she told me of the comfort she felt each morning when she heard "the first bird song of the day," after not sleeping all night; and the last kiss on the cheek from my father when I left him, not knowing it was the final good-bye. These memories assure me of the love that bonded us and held us close to one another. They continue to restore the connections for me.

I am reminded of Etty Hillesum's journal entry shortly before she was forced to leave her loved ones behind and go to a Holocaust camp:

I won't take any photographs of those I love; I'll just take all the faces and familiar gestures I have collected and hang them up along the walls of my inner space so that they will always be with me.[14]

Remembering the goodness of people has been a source of transformation for me. When I remember the generosity and kindness of others, I am deeply touched, overwhelmed by their ability to be so loving, challenged to be that kind of goodness myself. One person whom I often recall and whose memory challenges me is my great-aunt Ida. I lived with her for a time when I was in high school and even then, in my self-absorbed teen years, I sensed the beauty of her goodness. She always had a kind word for others and was unbelievably generous in her sharing of the basic essentials in life when she had so little for herself. I marveled often at her patience and her ability to go through the days with so much enjoyment of life. The taste of her sugar cookies and the sound of her laughter are always there in my memory of her.

I know a woman whose memory of her grandmother was a great source of healing for her. This woman was filled with strong anger over a work situation. She came to me and talked about her inability to move on and to let go of this. All she could think about was how much she hated those who had hurt her. I suggested that she take a day of prayer to get in touch with her negative feelings and to be with Sophia, to allow the truth of "what to do" to arise from within herself. I sensed that what she needed to do was to begin the process of letting go and forgiving those who had hurt her. When she returned, she told me that as she prayed she had a profound memory of her grandmother's kindness to someone who had hurt her grandmother deeply. She had not thought about this incident for over twenty years. As this surprising memory came back to her, she saw how forgiving and kind her grandmother had been to someone in need. It was then that she felt the pull to begin forgiving those at work. She said to me, "If my grandmother could be so kind, I want to do the same. I know that it will take time, but I will keep returning to this memory because it gives me so much courage."

I find it especially valuable to pull out my inner photo album when I am going through life's struggles. One good memory can carry me through a tough situation like a sturdy ship on a rough sea. The gift of remembering can clear the air inside of me and give me a better perspective of what is happening. During the struggling times, I can so easily forget all the good things that have been a part of my life. Good memories can draw me away from depression, doubt, and anxiety and can turn me around to face some of the joys and blessings that are there mixed in with all the pain.

Sometimes something external can trigger a treasured memory and take me inside to where light and happiness dwell. One external item that I have is an old jar that used to hold honey. I took it with me on a retreat in Colorado. Each day while I was there, I would take a piece of bread and this old jar filled with water in my backpack. I would spend the day in the mountains with this nourishment. The last day coming down the trail, I decided to collect a few things to help me remember those blessed days. I picked up a small stone, a little piece of bark, a flower, and a pine cone and placed them in my empty jar. That was many years ago. Today I can look at its contents and easily remember the retreat and all its beauty.

Another external form for helping to recall treasured memories is the use of a journal. It has been a very valuable method for me of storing up memories and having them available for easy recall. I have kept a journal for many years, and I try to be faithful to daily entries in it. Because my life is so full, I tend to forget many of the people and events that energize my days. Noting these daily in my journal does not take long to do, and it truly gifts me when I read my entries each month. I am astounded at all the things I have forgotten. As I read and recall the treasured memories, I often see them in the light of John Houseman's "miracles," and I am filled with awe and gratitude.

Celebrations of birthdays and anniversaries and other gatherings also help me to remember and to ponder the growth that has occurred in my life. When I think life is too busy to gather with friends or to celebrate special events, then I know that I am no longer living with a heart of gratitude and joy. It is so easy to get caught up in a functional, productive, intense work-a-day world and to miss the beauty of life and the joy of love that significant people bring. Many times storytelling happens at these events. It enables those present to live again the treasured happiness of past days. In the year of my fortieth birthday, I decided to celebrate the gift of life rather than to bemoan the aging process. I gathered my family and friends from everyplace, and I shared with them some of my treasured memories through song, slides, and prayer. There was much joy and laughter that evening as my loved ones helped me to remember and to celebrate who I am.

Celebrating who we are is vital to a life lived with gratitude and a sense of daily miracles. The more we can see how wonderfully we are made, the greater will be our joy in life. One night I clearly saw the radiance and the wonders that lie within the human spirit. The moon was bright, filling the dark night with wonderful shadows and enough glimmer to walk along the beach in quiet communion with the sea. As I walked along silently, I looked at the beautiful homes along the shoreline. I had often walked past these homes in the daytime, and they seemed quite aloof and apart from me. I only saw the outside of the homes and rarely saw any activity of the people who dwelled within. On this night, however, I looked with wonder. Many of the houses had lights on in the rooms. I could see the occupants sitting there enjoying the evening. They looked cozy, contented, at peace. The rooms were spacious, colorful, with a great variety of furniture and artwork. They were filled with welcome and beauty.

The next day I thought about that special walk during which I felt so connected with the homes along the beach. I began seeing these homes as symbols of the human spirit. Most of what I usually see of any person is only the surface. Only rarely do I see inside of another, recognizing the spaciousness there or feeling the warmth and the light that fills the human spirit with beauty.

As I thought about this, I realized that we are much more wondrous than we could ever believe. We ourselves are a great storehouse of treasures waiting to be discovered. When we were conceived, when egg and sperm united, a vast world of memories united at that time: memories of the world's beginnings when Sophia was there, memories of the earth's turning and churning, memories of all our ancestors with their joys and sorrows, memories of the deep strain of life winning out over the death that tries to invade it. I saw so clearly that we human beings are treasured memories. And I saw that Sophia, the Star inside the heart of each person, is wonderfully lit and radiant. I saw Sophia delighting in her presence within each person, eagerly radiating her goodness there.

Now when I close my eyes and think of the ocean, I remember those wonderfully bright homes in the darkness, and my heart is filled with joy. Through the years Sophia keeps generously giving me deep looks at life. Each time she does so, there is more wisdom in my heart.

★

Here are some of the wisdoms that Sophia is sharing with me through the gifts of treasured memories:

★ The bonds of *love and friendship* that I have with others can be strengthened and sustained through my remembrances of them.

★ During the difficult and dark times in my life, it is helpful to recall my *past blessings* and moments of happiness. They remind me that life will not stay dark forever.

★ As I remember *loving people* I am drawn to transformation. The memory of their goodness creates a desire in me to have more of that goodness shine forth from the window of my own inner being.

★ Treasured memories are waiting there deep within me. As I recall them, I will be able to see my life filled with *daily miracles*, fashioning my heart into a vessel of gratitude.

Meeting Sophia

1. What are some of the treasures of your inner photo album? Has one in particular become a focus for you in your life, influencing your values and your lifestyle?

2. Gather your family/friends for a "treasured memories" celebration. Invite the group to share memories. For starters you might ask them to share:
   - a favorite place where they lived or traveled
   - a humorous incident from their youth
   - a person who has influenced their vision of life
   - a surprising event that brought them great joy and happiness

3. Choose one treasured memory to celebrate. You may wish to do this alone or with others. You could sing about it or draw it, write it out or tell it to someone, or use some other creative approach.

4. Make a treasured memory photo album. Choose your favorite photos. Jot down your happy events. Name the people who have been with you on your journey. Who and what have shaped your life and helped to create the person you are today?

5. Draw a mandala of your treasured memories.

6. Choose a scripture passage, perhaps one that you often find helpful or comforting. What does this passage remember about God?

CHAPTER SIX
THE OPEN WINDOW

*She Will Guide Me Prudently
in My Undertakings.*

WISDOM 9:11

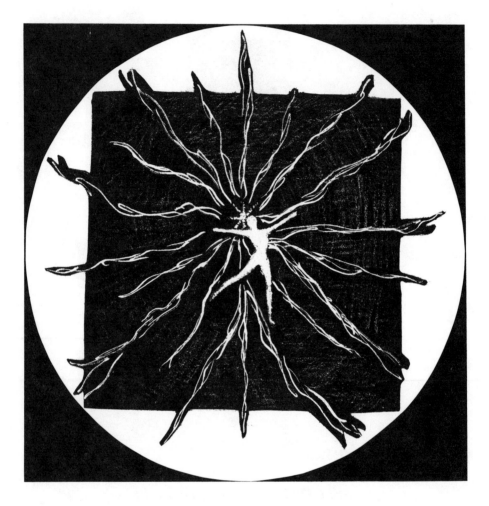

inside each of us
there awaits
a wonder
full
spirit of freedom

she waits
to dance
in the rooms
of our heart
that are closed
dark and cluttered

she waits
to dance
in the spaces
where negative feelings
have built barricades
and stock-piled weapons

she waits
to dance
in the corners
where we still
do not believe
in our goodness

inside each of us
there awaits
a wonder
full
spirit of freedom

she will lift light feet
and make glad songs
within us
on the day
we open the door of ego
and let the enemies
stomp out

— Joyce Rupp

61

As I was leaving for work one morning, I opened the door to the apartment and found a frightened, disoriented blackbird flying in the stairwell between the second and third floors. As it flew about in its search for freedom, the small bird kept hitting itself on the walls and the ceiling. I opened the hallway door to the next floor where there was an open window for the scared creature to fly out. I tried to shoo the bird toward the window, but it kept going back to the small stairwell space. As I hurried down the steps, I hoped that the panicky bird would find its way out. But that evening when I returned home, I sadly found an exhausted bird lying there, dead.

Later, as I reflected on my day, I thought about that dead bird. It was such a vivid picture of disorientation and unfreedom. The bird had no sense of a larger world. It had fixed its sights on that small space, seeing it as the only reality, and had missed the freedom of the open window. It was too caught up in its own fear and confusion to see a way out.

The blackbird reminded me of a scripture story with which I have often felt strangely connected: the man who was out of his mind and roamed among the tombs, gashing and hurting himself with stones. The story tells us that Jesus came and restored the man "to his senses" (Mark 5:1–20). I am not exactly sure why that story resonates so much with me. I think, perhaps, it is the part of me that yearns for inner freedom yet hides from it at the same time, the place in me that resists coming home to my truest self. It is in this unfree place that I hide from what will bring me to greater wholeness.

How can I resist the invitation to personal wholeness, to be my truest self, when I am always yearning for this in my life? Yet, I do resist it. There are times when I allow my fears, anxieties, or confusions to keep me from making a change in my life that would be for my growth. Sometimes it has been something rather simple, like trying on a new style of behavior. For example, I recognize this happening in me when my life and work call me to be in a "high extrovert" situation, meeting and greeting new people, entering into long hours of socializing and relating to strangers. The part of me that knows how delicious it feels to be an introvert wants to run and hide, to not reach out, to close my inner door and go home to solitude and quiet. But each time I fight my resistance to stay with my old introverted behavior, I have been greatly enriched by the people whom I have met. They help me discover the larger truths of life. They give a balance to my introversion; thus, I am more whole.

I have also had invitations to inner freedom when I have been in relationships that needed changing — either a change in attitude, such as offering forgiveness or understanding; or a move to terminate an unhealthy situation. Sometimes fears take over, and I hesitate making a decision because of all the "what ifs" involving hurt and confusion, even possible rejection and hatred from the other person. At times like this, my inner space has felt as confusing and constricting as the stairwell for the blackbird. I refuse to move toward the open door and window of communication and risktaking. Instead I fly and flutter around, bruising my spirit with my anxieties and concerns, or with my angry, hostile, and hurt feelings.

I think that there is a part of all of us that is like the small, scared blackbird. We yearn for an unknown something that will gift us with greater inner freedom and more wholeness. Yet, we are fearful of it because it is an unknown to us and foreign to our experience. When our fears and anxieties increase, our sense of our true self lessens. We become ruled by our strong hold on what we believe to be "the truth" of life for us. We, too, become disoriented and lose our way.

It is our ego, the "I" part of us, that gets in our way of inner freedom. Our ego thinks it knows everything. It likes to do things its own way, to have strong control, and to keep things in its confined, known space. It is our ego, so content and so clinging to the safe and to the secure, that fights with a fury against the true self who is trying so bravely to offer us the unknown truth. When the true self speaks up, lets itself be known, makes a move toward the open window, the ego tries to scare it off, makes it back down, and may even cause the true self to doubt its authenticity.

The ego gives many warnings and makes many excuses to the true self:

"You don't need to change."

"You've always done it this way."

"Look out. This will really bring you pain."

"Who do they think they are, anyhow?"

"It's the other person's fault."

"Stay with what you know and are sure of."

"Be careful. You'll probably fail."

We all need to have an "I" but we need a *healthy* "I." A healthy ego is one that knows there is a lot more truth than is presently seen or understood. It allows the true self to bring forth more truth and does not get defensive and territorial about it.

Sophia is our true self's best friend. She is a voice in the dark, a whisper of calm and courage amid the ego's strong voice of fear and clinging to security. As the ego fights to have its way, Sophia keeps moving the true self to the open window, offering clarity, insight, and vision. It is Sophia who gifts us with inner freedom. She does this, not just in the big moments of our lives, but every day as we search for the truth of who we are and how we are to live a life of wholeness. Sophia is always coaxing us to let go of our strong hold on what we think is the truth in order to accept what really is the truth.

One of the most helpful ways for me to be aware of the struggle for inner freedom is to be aware of the feelings and the messages that keep repeating themselves inside of me. I need to be intentional about being aware of what is going on inside of my spirit. I do this by listening to my feelings. They can tell me a lot about my motivations and my expectations, my wants and my needs. When I am aware of my motivations, I can find out what is pulling or pushing me to speak, to think, and to feel in a certain way. Listening to my inner messages — my "need to's, want to's, shoulds, ought to's, won'ts, can'ts, musts, have to's" — is just part of this process.

Some of my motivations might be: desire for success, need to be loved, lack of self-esteem, desire for other's good, greed, generosity, jealousy, envy, making an impression, having the final say, fear of failure, guilt, fulfillment of a dream, love of justice, compassion, hope for the future, belief in my goodness or the goodness of others. Motivations are many and varied, positive or negative. Whatever they are, they greatly influence my ability to grow in inner freedom.

Sometimes I ask myself questions in order to get at what my motivations and strong feelings might be, questions such as these:

Why am I so upset about this?

Where is this feeling coming from?

What makes me want this so much?

Who am I trying to protect?

What caused me to say what I did?

Do I care about the other person's wellbeing?

Am I being ruled or taken over by my feelings?

As I ask the questions, I go deep inside, to where Sophia dwells. This is where the glimmers of truth come. People often tell me that they are afraid to go inside of themselves for fear of what they might see there. I feel very differently about this because I often see the truth when I go inside. This is the beginning of greater freedom, if I am willing to wrestle with the truth which is being offered to me. It is not always clear at first. Sometimes I just trust my intuition and go slowly toward what appears to be the open window. It is helpful for me to have a good spiritual companion to check all this out so that I do not delude myself.

I remember a time when I discovered how ego-centered one of my good friends was. Just when I was at the point of thinking that I could hardly endure it anymore, I looked within myself and, to my great dismay, I saw that her egocentric approach to life was mirrored in my own. I discovered this by being attentive to the negative feelings within me, by seeing what caused my frustration and irritation, by looking at my expectations of myself and of her, and by talking with my spiritual companion.

This was a quiet, ongoing struggle for me. But most of our moves toward inner freedom do happen from day to day. If we are attentive to these inner moves and allow Sophia to draw our true selves to the open window, we will find that the major struggles toward inner freedom are easier to handle. We will not be so resistant to the truth because we know how good it feels to fly more freely.

One of the best things about inner freedom is the ability to be less controlled by our emotions or our ideas, to be able to sort them out and to see what leads to greater good. It is the gift of deliberately choosing to act in a certain way, not out of guilt, fear, coercion, manipulation, or any other unfree motivations, but because we want to do so. When we have inner freedom, we are able to dwell more quietly at our center because we are more true to who we really are. To be free inside is to know and to accept the person we are becoming. It is to have a vision of life and self that moves us toward goodness and wholeness, always drawing us into bonding with all that is good in our world. When our true self is freed, we are a blessing to others, often without realizing it, because the peace at our center comes through to the other.

Inner freedom does not always come easily. It asks a price from us. It often hurts to let go of what we thought was the truth. There is some necessary purification involved when we let go of the ego's strong need for security. We must be willing to pay the price for inner freedom. Part of the cost for this is our willingness to surrender to Sophia's guidance and direction, to trust that she knows the way through the darkness. Will we trust Sophia's presence and light? Will we deliberately and intentionally pause to reflect on our feelings and motivations? Will we let go of what keeps us from being our truest self? Will we choose to move toward what gives life and not just toward what gives security? These are Sophia questions, leading us toward greater inner freedom.

My trust in Sophia is always challenged in moments of turmoil and distress. Yet, at the same time, I grow ever more sure about Sophia's ability to help me gain inner freedom. Deep inside of me I know that Sophia draws me to what will bring me to greater life. She gives me strength to let go of my securities. She leads me to insights and to truths deep inside that give me greater freedom.

★

As Sophia keeps drawing me to the open window, she continually offers me wisdoms about inner freedom:

★ I must be *willing to change* and to grow if I am going to move to greater freedom. I need to be willing to look for the open window.

★ The *search* for truth is often *costly* because it means letting go of some of my feelings and ideas and ways of behavior which keep me from being my true self.

★ It is essential that I *recognize* my *feelings* and my motivations as I attempt to make good choices and decisions about my life.

★ Sophia, the truth-giver, is always ready to take me to the open window. To do so, she needs my *trust* and my *surrender*.

Meeting Sophia

1. Quiet your body, mind. Go to the center of your being. Picture an open window. Go and stand there, seeing Sophia standing there with you. Listen to what she speaks to you about your journey of life and the window. Quietly move from the window when you feel that Sophia is finished speaking. Write in your journal what Sophia shared with you. You may also want to write your response to her.

2. Sketch an open window. On or around the window write the truths that have led you to greater inner freedom during the past five years.

3. Take a day to be especially aware of your strongest feelings that day as well as your motivations: why you think, say, do what you do. At the end of the day, reflect on what you learned during the day about your inner freedom.

4. Read the reflection at the beginning of this chapter. What are the "enemies" that need to "stomp out" of your ego?

5. Play some of your favorite music. Be attentive to your true self. Give yourself to the dance of inner freedom.

6. What is your image of nonfreedom? Write it or draw it. What is your image of freedom? Write it or draw it. Share these images with a significant other.

7. Draw a mandala. Fill it with your true self as you see it full of freedom.

EPILOGUE

Go After Her and Seek Her;
She Will Reveal Herself to You;
Once You Hold Her, Do Not Let Her Go.
For in the End You Will Find Rest in Her
and She Will Take the Form of Joy in You.

ECCLESIASTICUS 6:27-28

Fireflies danced in the forest
while the summer stars
wove wondrous patterns
in the early night sky.

I sat on an old hollow log,
pondering my existence;
contemplation came easily
in that forest cradle of beauty.

A tender movement of recognition
swept across my soul;
clumps of tears rose up in me
as I perceived Sophia's stirring.

How good it felt
in that fleeting space
of starlit night;
how easily, then, to surrender.

I, who had known Sophia's presence
like some flickering firefly,
discovered she could not be captured
in the jar of my control.

On that starlit night
something in me gave way
opened up, let go,
and in that moment of surrender,
Sophia brought me home again.

— Joyce Rupp

Autumn came. I had promised to write a book on Sophia. I knew that I had to seriously begin considering what the content of the book would be. I felt some fear about how and where to start. I believed strongly in Sophia's presence and activity in my life, but it felt awesome to even begin to put all this into words. I knew, with the author of Ecclesiasticus, that I had gone after Wisdom, that I had sought her, but only because she had first sought me, had created a deep hunger in me for truth, beauty, goodness.

I was thinking these thoughts that late October morning as I walked in the early dawn. It was a mystical morning. There was a quiet mist and a gentle fog that shrouded the woods with an inviting veil of silence. It was in this contemplative moment that I met the owl. My heart leapt as I looked up and saw it sitting there on top of a road sign, just a few feet in front of me. I stopped instantly and gazed in disbelief at what I saw. The owl gazed back at me. I had never been so close to an owl. I stood there for a long time, absorbed in the silence and the beauty of the bird. The owl never moved but the eyes were focused on me. I felt a tremendous drawing to that silent figure. Something in me yearned to touch the soft feathers, to draw nearer to those large round eyes. Finally I took a small step toward the owl, and just that quickly the wide-winged bird lifted off silently and flew away.

I was not disappointed. I knew I could not stand there all day looking at an owl. I also knew the owl would probably not sit there all day looking at me. It had to come to an end. But all day long my heart sang in memory of seeing the owl. It sang the next day and the next. At times I would say to myself, "Did I really see that owl? Was I really that close?" And then I would sense all over again the tremendous drawing power of that moment. I will never forget the communion I felt in that simple, unexpected meeting of the owl. Since then I have often heard an owl's hoot in the late night or early morning. Whenever I have heard it, I have been immediately connected with the experience of that mystical October morning.

Was it mere coincidence that I should meet an owl as I began to write about Sophia? I do not know. I only know that the owl's presence became a special symbol for me as I wrote the pages of this book. The fears about what I would write left me after I met the owl. A sense of urgency filled me. I concentrated on the power of my unexpected meetings with Sophia. I could not wait to see what I would discover about Sophia as I pondered her presence in my life. I was constantly amazed. What I have discovered is that my meeting with Sophia has been as strong and as real as my meeting with the owl — and just as elusive.

Sophia has truly taken on the form of peace and joy in me. As I have written this book, I have had to go deep inside of myself. I have searched for words to describe my experience of this wonderful Star in my heart. Sometimes the words have seemed very elusive, but the experience has felt very real. This process has convinced me more than ever of the necessity to be still, to have solitude in this wild, fastly turning world in which I live.

The author of Ecclesiasticus speaks of Sophia and says:

If you love listening you will learn.
If you lend an ear, wisdom will be yours.
(Ecclesiasticus 6:23)

It is a challenge to remain faithful to this listening stance in my life. I realize that there is a vast treasure of truth which I have yet to discover. I believe that I have only begun to walk with Sophia and to enjoy the beauty of her starlight. The most significant thing is that the desire is there, the yearning to know and to grow.

It is also a challenge to live out the wisdoms which Sophia reveals to me. I believe that my life needs to reflect what has so graciously been given to me. Sophia would never lead one into a narcissistic and self-centered life. She is deeply connected and concerned with all the universe. She offers her wisdoms for the transformation of the earth. What she has given must be reflected and shared.

Sophia keeps calling to me. She is real. She is near. She does shine like starlight in my heart. I believe that she is there for you as well. As you leave the pages of *The Star In My Heart*, it is my hope that you will remain faithful to Sophia's presence. Often picture or image Sophia as the Star within you. Feel her blessed presence there, guiding and directing you. For she is, indeed, "more splendid than the sun; she outshines all the constellations" (Wisdom 7:29). Welcome her radiance. Believe in her light. Invite her truths into your life. Wait for her to reveal. Absorb what she shares. Integrate these wisdoms and let them live in you. May they be so vibrant that the starlight in you transforms the world around you.

There's a Star inside of me;
She shines there in my heart
and waits to be recognized.

Darkness tries to scare her off,
ego attempts to ignore her,
busyness pushes her around.
But this wonderful shining Star
keeps twinkling, all aglow.

She waits to lead me
to an unknown meadow
where the truth of who I am
will be revealed to me.

Shining Star, faithful Star,
when will I follow you?
When will I come to the meadow
where the truth will set me free?

— Joyce Rupp

Bibliography

Bergant, Dianne, CSA. *What Are They Saying About Wisdom Literature?*. Mahwah, NJ: Paulist Press, 1984.

Bolen, Jan Shinoda. *Godesses In Every Woman*. San Francisco: Harper and Row, 1984.

Brewi, Janice and Anne Brennan. *Celebrate Mid-Life*. New York: Crossroads, 1988. (c.f. Part IV, "Emerging Wisdom and Full Life: Wisdom as Archetypal").

Cady, Susan, Marian Ronan and Hal Taussig. *Wisdom's Feast*. San Francisco: Harper and Row, 1989.

Campbell, Joseph with Bill Moyers. *The Power of Myth*. New York: Doubleday and Co., 1988.

Caprio, Betsy. *The Woman Sealed In The Tower*. Mahwah, NJ: Paulist Press, 1982.

Carr, Anne E. *A Search for Wisdom*. Notre Dame, IN: University of Notre Dame Press, 1988.

Dunne, John. *The House of Wisdom*. San Francisco: Harper and Row, 1985

Eisler, Rianne. *The Chalice and the Blade*. San Francisco: Harper and Row, 1983.

Fiorenza, Elizabeth Schussler. *In Memory of Her*. New York: Crossroads, 1983. (c.f. pp. 130–140, "The Sophia-God of Jesus and the Discipleship of Women").

Fleming, Pat, Joanna Macy, Arne Naess and John Seed. *Thinking Like A Mountain*. Philadelphia/Santa Cruz: New Society Publishers, 1988.

Gray, Elizabeth Dodson. *Patriarchy as a Conceptual Trap*. Wellesley, MA: Roundtable Press, 1982.

Houston, Jean. *The Search For the Beloved*. Los Angeles: Jeremy P. Tarcher, Inc., 1987.

Iglehart, Hallie. *Womanspirit: A Guide to Women's Wisdom*. San Francisco: Harper and Row, 1983.

McFague, Sallie. *Metaphorical Language: Models of God in Religious Language*. Philadelphia: Fortress Press, 1982.

O'Connor, Kathleen M. *The Wisdom Literature*. Wilmington, DE: Michael Glazier, 1988.

Plant, Judith (ed.). *Healing the Wounds*. Phildelphia/Santa Cruz: New Society Publishers, 1989.

Stone, Merlin. *When God Was a Woman*. San Diego: Harcourt Brace Jovanovich, 1976.

Swimme, Brian. *The Universe is a Green Dragon*. Santa Fe: Bear and Company, 1984.

Woodman, Marian. *The Pregnant Virgin: A Process of Psychological Transformation*. Toronto: Inner City Books, 1985.

Companion Tape to THE STAR IN MY HEART
She Is Wisdom, Sophia
Sophia Songs for Women to Sing Together
LYRICS: Joyce Rupp; MUSIC: Joelle Mauer; VOCALIST: Claudette McDonald

---

Notes

Thoughts from the Author
1. References in the Hebrew Scriptures which refer directly to Sophia: Proverbs 1:20–33; 3:18; 4:5–9; 8:1–36. Wisdom 6:12–17; 7:7–14; 22–30; 8:1–18; 9:9–11; 10:1–21; 11:1–26. Ecclesiasticus (also known as Sirach) 1:9–10,14; 4:12–18; 6:18–31; 14:20–27; 15:1–10; 24:1–29; 51:13–22. Baruch 3:29–38; 4:1–4.
   References to Wisdom or Sophia in the Christian scriptures are less frequent and more implied than specific. Some passages with more direct reference to Sophia are: I Corinthians 1:23,25; 2:6–9. Colossians 1:15–17. Ephesians 3:9–11, 15–22. James 3:13–17. In John's Gospel the word "Logos" was used in place of "Sophia."
2. There is an ongoing discussion among scholars as to whether or not Sophia is divine. As I have read and studied the wisdom literature, it seems evident that Sophia is the feminine face of God. This aspect was eventually lost due to a highly male-dominated culture and a church that was very fearful of the goddess traditions of the past. In the Hebrew scriptures Sophia is referred to as the "breath" of God; she is there when creation occurs; she is "pure emanation" of God, a description which gives her an intimate union with the Divine. (See the Scripture references listed in the first note above.)
3. Thomas Merton, "Hagia Sophia," *A Thomas Merton Reader*, edited by Thomas McDonnell (New York: Doubleday and Co., Inc., 1974), 508.

Chapter 1
4. Jessica Powers, *Selected Poetry of Jessica Powers*, edited by Regina Siegfried, Robert Morneau, (Kansas City, MO.: Sheed and Ward, 1989), 21.

Chapter 2
5. Ira Progoff, *The Well and the Cathedral* (New York: Dialogue House Library, 1971), 67.
6. Elizabeth Dodson Gray, *Patriarchy As A Conceptual Trap* (Wellesley, MA: Roundtable Press, 1982), 115.
7. Thomas Merton, *New Seeds of Contemplation* (New York: New Directions Books, 1961), 296–297.
8. Powers, *Selected Poetry*, 22.
9. Etty Hillesum, *An Interrupted Life: The Diaries of Etty Hillesum, 1941–43* (New York: Pantheon Books, 1981), 225.
10. Ibid., 154.

Chapter 3
11. William Bridges, *Transitions: Making Sense of Life's Changes* (Reading, MA: Addison-Wesley Publ. Co., Inc., 1980), 100.
12. Judith Viorst, *Necessary Losses* (New York: Ballantine Books, 1986), 3.

Chapter 4
—

Chapter 5
13. Viktor Frankl, *Man's Search for Meaning* (New York: Simon and Schuster, 1963), 57–61.
14. Hillesum, *An Interrupted Life*, 183.

Chapter 6
—

THE AUTHOR

Joyce Rupp, osm

Joyce is a member of the Servants of Mary community, a freelance writer and has been a retreat director for eighteen years. She received a B.A. degree from Duchesne College in Omaha and a M.R.E. degree from St. Thomas University, Houston, with studies in spirituality at Creighton University and Notre Dame. She lives in Des Moines, Iowa, where she divides her time between writing, spiritual direction, and conferences and retreats in the United States, Canada, and Africa. Besides writing for several periodicals, her two previous books are *Fresh Bread* and *Praying Our Goodbyes* (Ave Maria Press).

THE ARTIST

Judith Veeder

Judith has been interested in the arts, especially music, since early childhood. She attended the University of Minnesota, earning a B.A. degree in psychology with a minor in music and art. She received a B.F.A. degree in art and a master's degree in counseling, with graduate training in art therapy. She has taught art therapy at Drake University and works with all age groups combining the uses of art, music, and movement. The mandala has served as a primary form for self-growth in her workshops and in her own life. Judith lives in Des Moines, Iowa, with her husband and two daughters.

Advance Reviews for THE STAR IN MY HEART

"Joyce Rupp challenges us to go deep within, to make friends with our fears, and to meet 'the star' in our hearts."
Marie Micheletto,rsm, Psychotherapist

"Reading Joyce Rupp's new book is like entering a vibrant circle dance that bows to the center of the psyche and pirouettes out toward the stars."
Bill Fitzgerald, Author of *Beyond Easter* and *Arrow and the Circle*.

"Warm, open, and sensitive. Rupp's practical and creative suggestions for meeting Sophia in our own hearts will go a long way in healing the sons and daughters of the patriarchy and bringing balance into our lives and culture."
Barbara Baker, Psychotherapist

"Joyce Rupp invites us to reflect upon our experience of life and offers us practical ways to acquire wisdom. The chapters on letting go and the healing of memories are worth the price of this book. Listening to what is in our heart, we enter into the heart of everyone, and we recognize the voice of *Wisdom*."
Al Bischoff,sj, University Pastor, Xavier University, Cincinnati, Ohio

"What a wonderful resource for those who know Sophia and want to enrich their relationship with her! Joyce Rupp shares her experience of Sophia as guide and companion."
Susan Cole Cady, Co-author of *Wisdom's Feast* and a United Methodist Pastor in Philadelphia

"The author helps readers discover within themselves Sophia's quiet companionship with all her goodness and constancy."
Janet R. Baumgartner, Saint Philip Parish, Battle Creek, Michigan

"Rupp has the rare gift of recognizing wisdom when she sees it. As in her earlier works, she uses that gift to lead us toward a deepening of our spiritual awareness. This book is spiritual direction of the best sort."
A. Arthur Schmidt, M.Div., Director of Mission and Ministry, Director of Clinical Education, St. Joseph Hospital and Health Care Center, Tacoma, Washington

If you enjoyed THE STAR IN MY HEART,
you'll value these other LuraMedia books:

CIRCLE OF STONES
Woman's Journey To Herself
by Judith Duerk

OVER 150,000 COPIES SOLD!

A guide for women searching for their inner wisdom. A personal yet universal journey to the essence of the feminine. Used in women's groups, retreats, and workshops all over the country. $11.95.

I SIT LISTENING TO THE WIND
Woman's Encounter Within Herself
by Judith Duerk

The second book in the CIRCLE OF STONES SERIES. Explores the inner masculine. A guide for women everywhere who are searching for their true selves in a world of changing values and roles. $11.95.

FINDING STONE
A Quiet Parable and Soul-Work Meditation
by Christin Lore Weber

An invitation to join Finding Woman on a journey to find your Stone of healing, wisdom, and power. A book to be savored slowly, in the tradition of ancient meditative practice of standing before life's mysteries. $12.00.

LuraMedia books are available in bookstores,
or call 1-800-FOR-LURA to order.
Ask for our free catalog!